PIUS XII

THE LIFE AND WORK OF A GREAT POPE

PIUS XII

The Life and Work of
a Great Pope

MGR PIERRE PFISTER
Canon at the Lateran

THE STUDIO PUBLICATIONS INC.

in association with

THOMAS Y. CROWELL COMPANY

NEW YORK

NIHIL OBSTAT
Carolus Boyer S.J., Rev. Deleg.
Romae, die 5 mensis Augusti 1954

IMPRIMATUR
✠ Aloysius Traglia
Archiep. Caesarien. Vicesgerens.
E Vicariatu Urbis, die 5 mensis Augusti 1954

NIHIL OBSTAT
Joannes M. T. Barton, S.T.D., L.S.S.
Censor Deputatus .

IMPRIMATUR
E. Morrogh Bernard, Vic. Gen.
Westmonasterii, die 28a Januarii, 1955

The sooner one comes to Rome,
the sooner it becomes part of one.

AN ILLUSTRATED BOOK ON ROME is irresistible and few there are who will not take it up and browse through it. It realizes the dream of those who hope one day soon to have the good fortune of contemplating the wonderful city in all the beauty of its proportions and its warm light. Or perhaps it reawakens the feelings of those who have spent unforgettable hours there, wandering along those streets where the history of thirty centuries lies beneath one's feet, and the landmarks are the names of emperor and pope, scholar and martyr, artist and saint.

This album would indeed like to extend an invitation, point out, or recall a memory. But still more it would like to lend power to that voice of Rome which speaks to the soul, replying untiringly to the questions of the curious, and bringing life and precision to their emotions; it is a voice that may speak from the lips of an obliging compatriot, be he student or monk, professor or prelate, met by happy chance, who becomes straightway a fast friend. You will never forget him, for his love for Rome reaches out to yours, and becomes its companion and mentor. He may or may not be a citizen of Rome in fact, but by the grace of God he is a very citizen of Rome; he feels it his duty to know all about the city, learning all that he can, and in loving it he loves those who love it too.

This friend cannot resign himself to being the friend of a single day. We meet him again in these pages which each pilgrim would have wished to be more numerous in his Journal; recording every step, every arresting vision, every mysteriously felt emotion, but his days at Rome, so grudgingly counted out, so fleeting, gave little time to write.

We meet him again in these pictures, which, carefully selected from many more, one would also have liked to collect for oneself. He keeps reminding us: "Don't lose a single detail of all this splendour. You will find in it that vision whose radiance, like a ray of grace, will be one of the guiding-stars of your life." It is his voice that above all one must listen to, for in displaying the history and traditions of Rome it reveals a deeper meaning behind these pictures. It alone can help you to see the true spiritual nature of Papal Rome behind what is outward and here to be seen. The pictures that follow, some of them showing ceremonies that only take place very infrequently, may be compared to a film that records a complete lifetime at Rome.

Usually books on art try to avoid showing figures of individuals in connexion with monuments as costumes and fashions date so quickly. But the works of art which form the background of the solemn functions presided over by the Sovereign Pontiff have no other *raison d'être* than these very sacred rites themselves. These are their life, and in this life during the course of so many centuries nothing has changed, nothing has grown old, and nothing has gone out of fashion. The great buildings that are seen here pay tribute to the Church's long history and to the original promise made to St Peter and his successors. Nothing is temporary or provisional; every possible form of art is utilized to make these ceremonies unrivalled in splendour. Procedure is scrupulously laid down and is based on the liturgy and etiquette. That is why pilgrims and experienced travellers always try to come to Rome when there is to be one of the great festivals, in the hope of taking part in one of the papal services; they know it will be a rewarding experience. This book on Rome and Pius XII attempts to bring together many different aspects of the presence of the Holy Father and of this beautiful and holy city

6

so that the reader can as he desires re-live his memories or travel there afresh in his thoughts.

★
★ ★

There are people everywhere in these troubled times who look towards Rome, and perhaps the Roman Church has never at any other time attracted as much attention as she does now, when every word or action of the Pope arouses interest all over the world. Messages of sympathy and admiration come to the Church from unexpected quarters and there is evidence that many place great hope in her. It seems that not only her faithful followers but others too look to her for standards and measure the extent of scientific achievement and destruction accordingly. In fact truth, justice, holiness, all that is of a higher order, spiritual and divine is in Rome visible, tangible and palpable. The world should rely more on this great moral power which restrains by saying: "*Non licet. Non possumus.*—It is not allowed. We cannot", and encourages with the words: "God wills it".

What other city has survived like Rome? The Roman Church too is very ancient, but is always young in spirit. She disowns none of her past but rather displays it with the aid of the finest archaeological and historical research. Her archives are open to all who wish to consult them. With jealous care she guards the divine trust of her founder and draws upon resources that are of their nature ever new. Her doctrinal decisions, which she considers to be infallible, bind her into a unity where there is no possibility of error. By her unchangeable dogmas and principles she perpetuates the past without being chained by it. Guarding the treasure of her dogmas intact she develops their contents, specifies the wording and insists on belief; an example is the recent announcement about the dogma of the Assumption of the Blessed Virgin Mary, Mother of Christ. She admits in her ritual the practice of name patronage and devotions

7

and gives as examples her saints and their heroic virtues. Recently there have been simultaneous canonizations of a contemporary pope, a martyr missionary, a young man, two priests who had founded or revived congregations and a woman who had founded a work of charity, saints whose lives cover a period of more than two centuries.

In a world where everything passes so quickly this endurance of the Church is quite remarkable. She it is who has kept Rome alive; building her out of the stones of the past, and quickening her with the life of nations. What it is to have such a long and beneficent past! And the Church has done more than endure; she gives proof that she lives, lives and gives life. Her relations with societies and races show all the suppleness of life that has no fear of death. She does not rely on human ability which results only in broken pacts and the failure of alliances.

For the Church endurance has meant life and this always in Rome, a city famous for its ruins of bygone magnificence. One might say they had been left by providence to provide a contrast to the vitality of Christianity. What great significance they assume when seen in that light. These pagan monuments are the remains of a time that is past and will not return: powerful as they may still look, they are only ruins or foundations: Etruscan stone, royal tufa and imperial marble; plinths of statues and majestic steps of temples that no one climbs any more. But the Church is neither a ruin nor a subject for archaeology. Her temples are not museums where beautiful objects are displayed for the pleasure of the onlooker. Her monuments are inhabited dwelling-places, sanctuaries that are frequented. They show Christian life today as a constant continuation of what it was in the past, and will be in the future. It is a heart-warming and very moving thought.

This life is revealed above all in the Church which is the Mother and Head of all the Churches, in this Eternal City; mother of virtue, mother of light and hope, mother also of all peace, of all joy, she is inspired by God to alleviate human misery with strength and comfort. This life, this spiritual and moral force, this teaching doctrine, this speaking authority is visible in the form of one man, the Pope; Representative of God, Sovereign Pontiff, Universal Teacher, Master of life and soul, Bishop of Rome.

Rome is so much the seat of the Pope that to say Rome or to say the Pope is almost the same thing. Rome has spoken when the Pope has spoken. And unceasingly he defines points of doctrine, blesses, judges, governs and directs. Hence the influx to Rome of thousands of pious pilgrims from all parts of the world, who regard it as their spiritual home. Rome is already on the road which leads to the Roman Church, and the road at this time is trodden more than ever before. Once pilgrims had a great deal of time at their disposal and they spent much of it in prayer and in wandering from monastery to monastery and from parish to parish. Today they have to cherish their time and they cannot afford to stay long. When they are still far away they fall on their knees at the sight of the dome of St Peter's with the eternal cross on top: sons of the Church, they enter Rome like children whose father's house has been opened to them. They are sure to go to the Catacombs to recapture the vigour and courage of the first missionaries; they touch the tombs of martyrs and saints with their foreheads: they go the traditional round of the Seven Churches and everywhere they hoard impressions of this great labyrinth, whose secrets they would so dearly like to understand. They engrave in their memory the names of hills, streets, churches and palaces which afterwards they talk of as their own homes and property. In the ancient basilicas and in other churches they teach one another, and, shoulder to shoulder with brothers of all races and of all lands, they sing the same triumphal *Credo* and piously take part in the beautiful liturgical ceremonies.

But they have really come to honour the Prince of Apostles. It is St Peter's that calls them to Rome. They always look at the windows of the Pope's apartments in the Vatican Palace with most awe, for there lives the Father of all the faithful, the Most Holy Father, he whom God has destined to be the living representative of mercy and justice and has

9

crowned with the crown that is always shining. And standing here at the entrance to the Palace they feel themselves to be sons of the city and cry "Here, with the Pope, we are at home". The Bronze Gate studded with iron does not frighten them; they have heard of it before. Once the Clock Gate, it has always led in to the House of the Universal Father, and was moved to its present position by Alexander VII in 1656.

Everyone, whether he is a Roman or a tourist, longs to penetrate the millennial mystery of the old palace and reach the foot of the pontifical throne, the central point of all the gathered crowds; and to get a place at a papal ceremony or the favour of an audience; to see the Pope, to throw themselves down before the Vicar of Jesus Christ, the Vicar of Love, and to lift their eyes from the shining whiteness of his soutane to the contemplation of his face. In its radiant goodness and kindliness it resembles the haloed pontiffs portrayed in early mosaics.

In 1895 Ollé-Laprune described his feelings about the Pope in the following timeless words:

"In the Vatican at Rome, adjoining St Peter's, lives the Pope. In him is expressed the whole Church, its duration and its life, its power and its beneficence. When he speaks or acts it is in the interests of truth and justice that he does it and in the name of God, who is all-knowing and above time and place. Outwardly the Pope appears to have little power, but in reality his strength is greater than anything on earth, for it is based on spiritual ideas that are clearly evident. He is the interpreter and minister of God, but a man, who has to work and suffer in order to fulfil his duty. In one sense he is detached from the results of his work, for often he sows what he will not reap; yet in another way he is determined that it shall go on, for even if he is mortal his work is immortal. He realizes that he must not get downcast; what he does not see, his successor will.

"The Pope is essentially all of this, by virtue of his office alone, but in addition his character inspires respect. He is the Pope, the supreme Father. How can one express the feelings that people have towards him, when in him are found the spirituality and holiness that give him the moral strength to fulfil his office? How serene is his presence! What courage he inspires! He combines nobility with perfect simplicity, decided opinions with forceful speech; there is nothing commonplace about him, every word, look or gesture seems exactly right and full of meaning, satisfying at the same time as it encourages one to look for deeper significance; finally, what majesty and what gentleness! He gives the impression of a being in perfect harmony with himself, who is both venerable and fatherly in his loving care. The present Pope is both a great man and a saint, who is not content with what he is but ever strives to be more saintly. He is one of the finest people that one could ever hope to see, and when one has had that great honour and joy one feels incapable of ever forgetting it. One feels ready to do anything to pass on his life-giving effect."

This moment before the Pope, the supreme aim of any pilgrimage, must surely come. And at that moment, proud and happy, touched to the depths of one's being, one can only say, "Most Holy Father". He will lean slightly towards you and say, "My child (*Figliuolo*), we bless you and all who are dear to you, and all that you have in heart and mind." His arms stretch out in prayer; then, after clasping his hands in front of him as if to draw infinite treasure from his heart, his right hand—this hand which for centuries has had the power to bind or loose—is raised swiftly to make the sign of the Cross, to bless the universe and consecrate it to God. Afterwards you will say that this was the most impressive moment of your life: "We have been blessed by the Crucifix."

The following page is one of the most precious pages in this book. It is the text of a letter by His Holiness Pius XII to the episcopal body of the United States of America in 1948. It is now beautifully engraved in marble as a monumental inscription, in order that all may read it

TO OUR BELOVED SONS, THE CARDINAL ARCHBISHOPS, AND TO OUR VENERABLE BRETHREN, THE ARCHBISHOPS, BISHOPS, AND LOCAL ORDINARIES OF THE UNITED STATES OF AMERICA HAVING COMMUNION WITH THE APOSTOLIC SEE

PIVS PP. XII

BELOVED SONS AND VENERABLE BRETHREN

THE APPROACHING REESTABLISHMENT HERE IN OUR DEAR ROME OF THE NORTH AMERICAN COLLEGE THE KNOWLEDGE OF WHOSE REOPENING HAS BEEN COMMUNICATED TO US BY THE RECTOR, AFFORDS US THE WELCOME OPPORTUNITY OF ADDRESSING OUR PATERNAL WORDS TO YOU, THE MEMBERS OF THE HIERARCHY OF THE UNITED STATES. WE REJOICE NOT ONLY IN THE FACT THAT AFTER A LAPSE OF EIGHT YEARS YOU ARE ONCE MORE SENDING YOUR CHOSEN YOUNG MEN TO STUDY IN OUR BELOVED CITY, TO IMBIBE THE SACRED WISDOM OF HOLY MOTHER THE CHURCH AT ITS VERY SOURCE, AND TO BE NOURISHED AT THE VERY HEART OF THE CATHOLIC WORLD, BUT THAT YOU ARE ALSO PLANNING TO ERECT IN THE VERY SHADOW OF OUR OWN DWELLING A NEW AND GREATER SEMINARY TO CARE FOR EVER MORE YOUNG LEVITES FROM AMERICA. IT WAS OUR PREDECESSOR OF BLESSED MEMORY, PIUS IX, WHO NEARLY ONE HUNDRED YEARS AGO FIRST PROPOSED TO THE AMERICAN BISHOPS THAT THEY ESTABLISH A NATIONAL SEMINARY IN ROME, AND IT WAS THE SAME PONTIFF WHO PURCHASED AND GRACIOUSLY GRANTED THE USE OF THE EDIFICE THAT HAS HOUSED THE AMERICAN STUDENTS EVER SINCE THAT TIME.

SURELY THERE IS EVIDENT THE HAND OF DIVINE PROVIDENCE IN THE FACT THAT THE FIRST STEPS WERE TAKEN ON THE OCCASION OF THE DEFINITION OF THE DOGMA OF THE IMMACULATE CONCEPTION AND THAT THE COLLEGE ITSELF WAS OPENED FOR THE FIRST TIME ON THE VERY EVE OF THE FEAST ON DECEMBER 7TH 1859, AND SINCE THAT DAY OUR HEAVENLY MOTHER, QUEEN OF THE CLERGY, HAS NEVER CEASED TO BLESS WITH EVERY MANIFESTATION OF DIVINE FAVOR A WORK THAT IS OF NECESSITY SO CLOSE TO HER MATERNAL HEART, THE STUDENTS NURTURED IN TENDER LOVE OF THEIR MOTHER AND QUEEN, DEVELOPED IN THE IMAGE OF HER DIVINE SON, ENLIGHTENED IN THE SACRED SCIENCES LEARNED AT THE FEET OF CHRIST'S VICAR, MADE STRONG AND COURAGEOUS BY THEIR CLOSE ASSOCIATION WITH THE PLACES SANCTIFIED BY THE PRINCE OF THE APOSTLES AND THE MARTYRS, HAVE RETURNED TO THEIR OWN COUNTRY TO WIN EVER GREATER TRIUMPHS FOR CHRIST AND HIS HOLY SPOUSE AS PASTORS AND TEACHERS, AS ADMINISTRATORS AND ALSO AS BISHOPS OF THE CHURCH IN AMERICA. THE MEN TRAINED HERE HAVE ALWAYS BEEN MARKED WITH AN ESPECIAL LOYALTY TO US AND TO OUR ILLUSTRIOUS PREDECESSORS, AN INEVITABLE CONSEQUENCE OF THEIR SOJOURN IN THIS CITY, THE SEE OF PETER AND OF PETER'S SUCCESSORS.

TODAY AS WE LOOK ABOUT THE CITY OF ROME WE SEE ON ALL SIDES THE FLOWER OF THE YOUTH OF THE WORLD, EVEN FROM THE MOST DISTANT NATIONS DRAWN HERE BY A COMMON FAITH, SUSTAINED BY COMMON IDEALS BEING TRAINED IN THE SAME DOCTRINE, SHARING THE SAME DIVINE SACRIFICE, AND ALL UNITED BY THE SAME BONDS OF ATTACHMENT TO US. SURELY THEY ARE GIVING TO THE LEADERS AND TO THE PEOPLES OF EVERY LAND A MAGNIFICENT EXAMPLE OF UNITY AND OF THE ABILITY OF MANKIND TO LIVE TOGETHER IN CHRISTIAN PEACE AND CONCORD. THE CONCURRENCE OF SO MANY THOUSANDS OF MEN, LATER DESTINED TO PLAY SUCH AN IMPORTANT PART IN THE SALVATION OF SOULS OVER THE WHOLE FACE OF THE EARTH, IS A GREAT CONSOLATION TO US AND IT SHOULD BE TO YOU, BELOVED SONS AND VENERABLE BRETHREN, A REASON ESPECIALLY APPEALING AT THIS TIME TO BE PROMPT IN MAKING EVERY SACRIFICE NECESSARY TO MAINTAIN AND EVEN TO ENLARGE THE NATIONAL SEMINARY OF YOUR COUNTRY.

SO IT IS WITH PARTICULAR JOY THAT WE HAVE LEARNED OF YOUR PROPOSALS TO ERECT AN EVEN FINER SEMINARY AND TO PLANT YOUR ROOTS EVEN CLOSER TO US. YOUR WISDOM AND COURAGE TO LOOK TO THE FUTURE AND TO PLAN FOR ALMOST THREE HUNDRED OF YOUR SEMINARIANS TO STUDY IN ROME REPRESENT A MOST WORTHY INITIATIVE THAT CAN ELICIT ONLY OUR WARMEST COMMENDATION. AT THE SAME TIME YOU ARE KEEPING A CLOSE TIE WITH YOUR OLD AND HONORED TRADITIONS IN PUTTING THE FORMER COLLEGE BUILDING TO USE AS A HOUSE OF STUDIES FOR PRIESTS WISHING TO TRAIN THEMSELVES IN THE HIGHER BRANCHES OF THE SACRED SCIENCES. BOTH OF THESE PROJECTS CALL FORTH OUR HEARTIEST APPROVAL AND SUPPORT AND THE RETURN IN GRACE AND WISDOM THAT WILL ACCRUE TO THE CHURCH IN AMERICA WILL AMPLY REWARD THE EXPENDITURES AND SACRIFICES THAT ARE NECESSARILY INVOLVED IN THEIR REALIZATION.

THE UNITED ACTION TAKEN IN THIS MATTER BY THE AMERICAN HEIRARCHY, ALWAYS SO READY AND GENEROUS IN THEIR SUPPORT OF ALL MEASURES FOR THE EXTENSION OF THE KINGDOM OF CHRIST, ONCE MORE DEMONSTRATES THE FLOURISHING CONDITION OF THE FAITH IN YOUR GREAT NATION. WE ARE SURE THAT THE BISHOPS AND PRIESTS AND PEOPLE WILL RALLY TO THE SUPPORT OF A CAUSE THAT PROMISES SO MUCH FOR THE CHURCH AND WHICH IS SO CLOSE TO OUR OWN HEART. ALREADY AN ABUNDANT AND FRUITFUL HARVEST FOR GOD AND FOR SOULS HAS BEEN GARNERED FROM THE PAST EIGHTY-NINE YEARS OF THE EXISTENCE OF THE NORTH AMERICAN COLLEGE, AND NOW YOUR DECISIONS FOR THE FUTURE GIVE ABUNDANT HOPE THAT SUCCEEDING GENERATIONS WILL CONTINUE, IN GREATER MEASURE AND WITH MORE AMPLE FACILITIES, TO ENJOY THE RICHEST BLESSINGS STEMMING FROM A PRIESTHOOD NOURISHED IN THE ETERNAL CITY. WITH GREAT JOY THEN WE GIVE OUR BLESSING TO THE PLANS THAT HAVE BEEN MADE KNOWN TO US BY THE RECTOR FOR THE FUTURE OF YOUR SEMINARY. WE SHALL FOLLOW THEIR UNFOLDING AND THEIR REALIZATION WITH INTIMATE PLEASURE AND PERSONAL INTEREST AND, AS A TOKEN OF OUR ENCOURAGEMENT IN THE GREAT TASK THAT LIES AHEAD, WE IMPART TO YOU BELOVED SONS AND VENERABLE BRETHREN, AS ALSO TO THE PRIESTS AND FAITHFUL OF THE UNITED STATES, OUR PATERNAL APOSTOLIC BENEDICTION.

GIVEN AT THE VATICAN ON THE EIGHTEENTH DAY OF FEBRUARY ONE THOUSAND NINE HUNDRED AND FORTY EIGHT, THE NINTH YEAR OF OUR PONTIFICATE.

PIVS PP. XII

PIVS·XII·PONT·MAX·HAS·AEDES·PRAESENS·DICAVIT·PRID·ID·OCT·A·MCMLIII

Inscription at the North American College in Rome

forever, the living and immortal word, and forms the most attractive ornament on the main floor of the new North American College in Rome. What a magistral lesson of the love of Rome was evoked by the Holy Father, when he said in this paragraph:

"Today as We look about the City of Rome We see on all sides the flower of the youth of the world, even from the most distant nations, drawn here by a common faith, sustained by common ideals, being trained in the same doctrine, sharing the same Divine Sacrifice, and all united by the same bonds of attachment to Us. Surely they are giving to the leaders and to the peoples of every land a magnificent example of unity and of the ability of mankind to live together in Christian peace and concord. The concurrence of so many thousands of men, later destined to play such an important part in the salvation of souls over the whole face of the earth, is a great consolation to Us; and it should be to you, Beloved Sons and Venerable Brethren, a reason especially appealing at this time, to be prompt in making every sacrifice necessary to maintain and even to enlarge the national seminary of your country."

This passage contains the essence of a later address by the Holy Father on April 16, 1953, to the pupils and former pupils of the French Pontifical Seminary; other students were present, privileged indeed to be making their studies at Rome. The Holy Father said:

"The importance and the special significance of Rome, you believed in and realized even before coming to the Eternal City; but you have proof now from your own eyes, and every day you enter more deeply into its meaning as you are pervaded with her teaching, her history and her spirit. When you come to the Vatican Basilica to venerate St Peter and to pray for his blessing on your priesthood, you find in the very grandeur of the fabric, in its artistic

13

adornments, in those vital texts which are blazoned on the great golden frieze of nave and dome a whole treatise 'de Romano Pontifice'. The most eloquent voices of tradition call you, in the words of St Cyprian, to love ever more 'that see of Peter, that first among the churches, whence the unity of the priesthood draws its origin'. (S. Cypriani Ep. LIX *c.* 14—Ed. Hartel, *Corp. Script. Eccl. Lat.* vol. 3, p. 2,683). The nearer one comes to the hearthfire, the stronger and the purer its glow. Similarly, close to the supreme authority of Holy Church, the age-old wisdom which must direct the exercise of the priesthood sinks more easily and more deeply into mind and heart. Make good use, beloved sons, of the precious years you spend in Rome. And, although they must remain your chief care, do not be content with intellectual labours alone. Her monuments, her institutions, the memory of so many saints who have walked the same streets as you, prayed in the same churches, exercised the priestly ministry to which you are called, all have their lessons for you; and nowhere else will you find them gathered together in such abundance."

How can one describe the rewards of those who obey the Holy Father? They no longer live only in the present; something within them thrills to the glory of the past, to a refrain that springs from art and history and is untroubled by the turmoil and wreck of civilizations. Starting in the earliest days of Rome, this chant carries on and the assaults of barbarism only seem to give more depth to the music. Their outlook broadens to include the whole of time; they see the results that the Papacy has had in the world, and as nothing yet has been able to overthrow its power they conclude that nothing ever will. The world will always receive good at the hands of Rome.

From the moment of one's arrival, it is not necessary to travel far afield to see Rome in her eternal reality. On the road, those highways of Rome, which from the Golden Milestone radiate over all Europe the traveller is seized and led on by history: the burial monuments herald the Gates of the City, which in the past were opened to many illustrious personages. Coming by air the first things that are visible as the aircraft comes down are the aqueducts—reminders that the ancients too used power to help in everyday life. Coming by rail one arrives at the great Terminus, a modern building which is perfectly adapted to its function and which happily is quite different from any of the old monuments. It seems the meeting-place of the old and the new; in fact the glazed canopy was designed to avoid the ruins of the city wall, built by Servius Tullius when he was king of Rome in the sixth century B.C. and strengthened after the Gallic invasion of 390 B.C. And suddenly one has to accept that legend still lives on in the present. Opposite, on the other side of the square, are the biggest Baths in Rome, which were opened in A.D. 305, a time when legend was giving way to history and paganism was coming to an end; Constantine was soon to come. According to one account this building "had its foundations and walls soaked in the sweat and blood of thousands of Christians. For seven years without a break they worked at the construction of the Baths, being treated with continual cruelty; they secretly marked a number of the bricks that they made with the sign of the Cross, not knowing that in so doing they were foretelling the future use of the building." The Baths were turned into a Carthusian monastery and later still into a museum; today this vast building contains a large church, Santa Maria degli Angeli, and in one of the four domed rotundas is the church of St Bernard, as big as the Pantheon. This perfect example of Rome's surprises and contrasts was explained by Cardinal Grente in the address he gave when he was installed at this church as successor to Cardinal Baudrillart and, before him, Cardinal Sarto, who later became Pope and is now known as Saint Pius X.

That is typical of Rome! You are still in the station square and there in front stretches a new world, an uncharted sea, a labyrinth reaching from the cave of the Lupercalia to brand new feats in reinforced concrete

15

—how is one not to get lost? A paper-boy shouts the latest news while around him the stones of Rome contain the history of the ages. A broad avenue lined with luxury shops turns into a narrow medieval alley in the course of a few yards. Façades of churches come right up to the edge of the pavement. On one side a narrow passage-way catches the eye and at the end can be seen a palazzo, as if at the end of a telescope. There are so many shrines, all dedicated to famous saints and all with fascinating relics or well-known pictures, that only those who have time to spare like the pilgrims of old can stop and examine them all. The art is mainly Baroque; a complete paradise of angels wrought in marble and gilt, supporting saints either in ecstasy or glory to give them a foretaste of the beatific vision. Who can truthfully say that he has visited all the churches in Rome—there are more than there are days in the year—and what is more, who can say that he has seen all the palaces, collections and museums? Don't risk going to the Vatican on foot or you may be detained on the way by too many fascinating details. For the streets of Rome are quite astounding; each stone seems to have something to say, and something important, whether it conjures up a memory or a prayer, or points a moral. In this city nothing is dumb, everywhere there are hidden links with the past. The men, too, are striking and recall descriptions of the senators of Ancient Rome with their fine build and stately walk. Young girls kneeling before images of the Madonna have the same features. And as well as all this, Rome is blessed with a sunny, temperate climate renowned for its cloudless days and wonderful light. People coming both from the north and from the tropics find that the weather is the equivalent of their mildest season.

Here let me give a word of advice. You have probably anticipated your first visit to Rome for a long time and have often looked at photographs of the city. If you are to get the full value of that first wonderful glimpse try to be quiet before you arrive and forget what you have heard about it before. Nothing will appear strange as a result, but everything will have just that extra freshness that will make it more new to you and alive.

The way to the Vatican lies past the bridge and Mausoleum of Hadrian (117–138). As one approaches it the Mausoleum and the Janiculum hill frame the dome of St Peter's which already catches the eye and fires the imagination. No one quite knows where the first founder of Rome lies buried. Under the Black Stone (*Lapis Niger*)? At the foot of *Roma Quadrata*, the early square city which tradition states was sited on the top of the Palatine hill? However that may be, St Peter died at Rome and, as its greatest benefactor, may well be considered the second founder of the city. Above his grave, later marked by the vast building and dome of St Peter's, a new era began; it continues to this day. From that grave came life. It was there that God completed the first link in a chain that has come down across nineteen centuries to the present day, making two hundred and sixty-one links in all. Statues of St Peter and St Paul stand at the end of the Ponte S. Angelo and above them on the top of the Castle stands St Michael sheathing his sword; he seems poised there to command the rows of angels carrying symbols of the Passion who line the bridge. They recall the vision of St Gregory the Great, who by his prayers obtained relief for Rome from the terrible plague of 590.

The sight from the top of the Avenue of the Conciliation is really magnificent. The eye is held by a double row of straight-sided, clean-cut obelisks that point towards the centre of the Basilica of St Peter's. The church is still over half a mile away, but it gives the effect of a cathedral altar at the end of a long nave. Could the builders have had this in mind? For since Holy Year this vast space has been used as an open-air church whenever congregations of hundreds of thousands have been expected for some very special ceremony. Lying between the River Tiber and the *passetto*, the covered passage-way between the Vatican and the Castle of

S. Angelo, the Avenue of the Conciliation is thus the centre aisle of this "greater" St Peter's; the piazza and the colonnades are the transept and the sky over Rome provides a perfect dome of deep blue. The parvis of St Peter's makes the sanctuary, and the façade itself and the dome a most wonderful reredos behind the altar of the papal throne. The Basilica itself might be considered the apsidal chapel. This idea came on the evening of the Canonization of St Pius X; some people who had been watching the immense crowd that stretched away as far as the eye could see to the Tiber, suddenly had the idea of going inside the Basilica to pay reverence to the shrine of the new saint. The building was deserted and already bathed in evening shadow and from outside came the sound of *vivats*. As His Holiness Pius XII was carried on the *sedia* towards the Portona di Bronzo, the whole of St Peter's echoed with the acclamations of the crowd.

The immediate surroundings of the Vatican have undergone few changes since Bernini built the Colonnade in front of the Basilica, except after 1870 in the large region covered by the Prati. All early travellers recorded their astonishment on first coming out of the narrow streets of the Borgo and seeing the huge building before them. Those who want to get an impression similar to that given in old accounts may go by the Borgo San Spirito or the Borgo Sant' Angelo. But one must not regret the many changes that one sees there today. Doubtless much had to be sacrificed to architectural symmetry, but then one does not understand why the wretched little streets had been left at all round the Vatican, the capital of the Roman Church and home of the Sovereign Pontiff. Besides, the restored façade of Santa Maria Transpontine and other modern buildings are already beginning to blend in with the old. The great Auditorium is used for assemblies over which the Pope sometimes presides, such as the jubilee concert of Mgr Perosi, the permanent Master of the Papal Choir. The palace of the Knights of the Holy Sepulchre is near that of the Eastern Church. Lastly there are two porches which stand out a little to mark the end of the avenue before the piazza begins;

18

this is the result of an architectural rule, which says that one open space must not abut upon another. This was also the reason for the avenue of obelisks, which break up the large open space. The solution had been debated for three hundred years and many projects had been put forward. Finally experiments and demonstrations were carried out in the presence of Pius XI, using collapsible hoardings to give the required effect. The chosen solution is in no way temporary and the completion of it was a major operation.

How many memories come to one when crossing the piazza in front of St. Peter's! It is well over three hundred yards across to the Portona di Bronzo or the Basilica. Do not forget that there are thirty centuries of history here beneath one's feet. The Etruscans held this area north of the Tiber for a long time and even afterwards not much was built there. There were a few roads coming from the end of the Pons Aelius, but otherwise there was nothing but graves. This was told us by legend, but has also been recently confirmed by excavations. When the old basilica was pulled down a humanist theory was started that the foundations of Constantine's basilica were really those of the Circus of Nero, but now it is recognized that this was situated much nearer the Janiculum, which was then separated from the Vatican area by a deep valley. Nero can never be forgotten at Rome, for his Gardens still exist. Each year on June 27th there is a procession to celebrate his first victims, the protomartyrs of Rome; it is a preparation for the solemn *Dies Natalis*, the anniversary of St Peter's death. On that day a large congregation goes to worship at his tomb, quite near the place where he confessed the Christ, once again crucified in the form of his Vicar.

There is no tradition or archaeological evidence to tell us where St Peter and the early popes lived. Theirs was the task of preserving the original teaching and trying to convert people during those bitter years of persecution. How blessed we would be if we could gather round them and hear their wise sayings! Their only permanent home seems to have been the grave, a pulpit from which they still continued to confirm people in the faith. "Trophies of the two Apostles", they were called by the theologian Caius, who said in invitation to Proclus the Montanist: "If you would like to come to the Vatican or drive along the Via Ostia you will find the trophies of those who by their teaching and courage established this Church on a firm footing." For 250 years the successors of St Peter had, written against their names: "Crowned martyr; buried near blessed Peter, in the Vatican", or "Via Appia, in the Cemetery of Calixtus". All that time and all those lives were necessary to convince the ancient world; all that time was needed to build the foundations of heavenly Rome on unshakeable rock. But still, God works in His own way and eventually He put an end to the Age of Martyrs; the Cross appeared in the sky and Constantine bore it with his eagles to the Temple of Jupiter on the Capitol, where he set it up. Later he had it placed on the Lateran and on the Apostle's tomb. From then on its gold shone forth unchecked despite all the assaults of the pagan world until the beginning of the seventh century. At that time St Gregory the Great was Pope and he thought that the end of the world had come; "My soul is tired of living", he is said to have cried. But St Gregory nevertheless did consolidate the work of Peter and Sylvester. Peace was established, Rome was relieved and good works were carried on. Pilgrims were given help, the Word of the Gospel was preached in distant lands and Christianity became finally established.

St Sylvester and Constantine noticed the steep slopes of the Vatican hill and the valley in front of it and they decided to erect a building that was worthy of the Cross of Christ and of Peter. It will always be said that it was an inspiration from On High that told His Holiness Pius XII to encourage scholars to reveal the shrine of St Peter once again free of all later masonry. As a result the people of today are satisfied, eager as they are for test and experiment. The days of belief are over; now one must see and touch with the finger. There is an old tradition that tells how Constantine brought twelve baskets of earth with his own hands at the start of work on the foundations of S. Salvatore in the Lateran, which was built on the site of a barracks and a palace. He is said to have done this also at St Peter's, which was built on the Vatican cemetery. In 1935 the paving stones of the Lateran basilica were taken up and the legend was explained; the ground floors of the two previous buildings had been filled in to raise the basilica and make it stand up above the city walls. Pius XI was delighted at the discovery, which revealed a trace of the times of the early apostles under the cathedral of Rome. Similarly it was later found that the Vatican cemetery had also been piled with earth up to the level of the stone on the top of St Peter's tomb; this was shown by excavating the neighbouring tombs. These two finds gave historians unexpected and irrefutable proof of the legend.

The Lateran was just about to be consecrated on November 9th, 327, when work began on the Vatican. It had the same basilical plan, so clearly thought out for the purposes of Christian liturgy by St Sylvester, and it also had the same dimensions (460 by 200 feet). These are the exact measurements of the Forum Romanum and it was fitting that the Christian forum should be the same size.

The history of its building and of its benefactions starts at the same moment. The earliest description of it is given by a writer of the fifth century, St Paulinus, when writing a comforting letter to his friend Pammachius. Pammachius' wife, the daughter of St Paula, had just died and on the same day Pammachius gave a great funeral feast to all the poor people of Rome. Paulinus recalls how they arrived in a serried throng "on the steps of the place and burst into the atrium, where the fountain plays, then on through the Royal gate, which glitters under a blue pediment". He describes the church as "a swarming hive of paupers", and gently observes that they are "the foster-children of divine love". Today the characteristics of the Vatican are much the same as in this first account. People who are hungry for the spiritual help and blessings of the Church hurry towards the welcoming basilica and there is no trouble that cannot find some solace from either the Holy Father or his Papal Alms-house, whose offices ceaselessly carry on their good works.

Similarly the Vatican station, which was built for the reception of the Pope's distinguished visitors, is now little more than an unloading point for a constant stream of gifts from all over the world, such as the cargo of cod-liver oil that came from Canada recently. Some of the many other things that arrive are medicines and clothes, and like everything else these are soon speeding away from the Vatican in trucks towards centres of poverty and distress.

The Pope does not only send material gifts, however; he also sends his chosen sons as Nuncios to the Governments of the world as ambassadors of peace and justice. They go to those who cannot come to the Pope, blessing them, teaching them and giving them advice; above all, they go where comfort is needed. It was in this capacity that Mgr Pacelli, the Archbishop of Sardis, was sent to the King of Bavaria at Munich by Benedict XV. It was the year 1917, a year of fire and pestilence, the third year of the Great War. He was sent to the front. In his advance position the Nuncio was like a far-flung outpost of the Holy See and his efforts for reconciliation and peace even reached the ears of Kaiser Wilhelm; but unfortunately this emperor could not hear the truth thus revealed by the messenger of God. The number of dead steadily rose; the number of graves became so great that a special service was created to identify them and give this small consolation to the families concerned. The Nuncio went to the cemeteries to offer up prayers for the families of the dead. In the prison camps conditions were bad and lack of food was undermining the health of the prisoners. The Papal Nuncio went round visiting them all, comforting them with a few words in their mother-tongue and bringing them gifts of clothes and rations. The thought that the Universal Father was thinking of them and doing something to help gave them patience to await the hour of peace. The Nuncio's charm was irresistible; at sight of him the weak took new courage, by his efforts condemned hostages were reprieved, sick prisoners were exchanged and refugees were looked after. After the war Constantinople erected a statue to the beneficence of the Papacy, dedicated as follows:

22

"To the great Pope Benedict XV, who at this tragic time in the world's history gave succour to the peoples of the world, no matter what their country or their religion, this statue is erected out of recognition and thanks." Who can number the services rendered to humanity by the Church, Our Most Holy Mother Church, in all the good works that she has started, organized and still promotes in the world!

One can get a better impression of what the old St Peter's was like by looking at S. Paolo fuori le Mura than by looking at old frescoes and crude medieval prints of the basilica. S. Paolo is one of the surviving basilicas built by Constantine and its beautiful proportions are noticeable the moment one goes in; the perfect ratio of height to breadth, the beauty of the pillars and the wonderful mosaics. It makes one slightly regret that the old St Peter's was ever destroyed.

So perfectly was the layout of the Christian basilicas adapted to the liturgy of the eucharist that it remained the standard form of Christian architecture right up until the development of the Gothic transept; it is striking proof of the unity of the early Church and its close connexion with the See of St Peter. Apart from baptistries and mausoleums, which were based on a circular plan round a font or a tomb, all the churches which were built after the Edict of Constantine followed the same general plan of having rows of columns on either side of the nave supporting the clerestory walls; in these upper walls there were tall windows which let in a flood of light all over the building. No other form of support was required. Even Santa Sophia, which was built two centuries later at Constantinople on the plan of a Greek cross with cupolas, was adapted to the Roman scheme of a double row of columns. Where marble was not available the craftsmen worked in the local stone, fashioning the columns out of cylindrical drums to give the same effect. Fire was the prime enemy of the early basilicas and it nearly always started with the wooden ceilings and beams. To remedy this Roman architects adopted the vault; this was very much heavier and the columns had to be strengthened to bear the weight, altering the traditional shape as little as possible. Notre Dame de Paris and the other early Gothic cathedrals used pillars very similar to those in the Roman basilicas, with the lower portion carved to give the appearance of columns. It was only above the capital that the Gothic architect risked a new departure and led the way to soaring ribs and high vaults; a clear proof of the desire to have Rome as base and foundation. Calixtus II, a Burgundian pope, celebrated his victory over the question of Investitures by building the basilica of S. Crisogono in Trastevere, in pure basilica style. These are all examples of the extraordinary consistency of the Roman Church up to the Renaissance, which was only due to the care with which every possible disturbing influence was kept at bay.

The great basilicas were constantly used and continually had to be restored. In 1452 St Peter's had just been completely redecorated, despite the ominous way in which the south wall was beginning to lean outwards, when Nicholas V decided to start work on a much bigger church. He named it after the Via delle Fondamenta, the road which went round the end of the apse; the foundations exist to this day. In the following year Mahomet II took Constantinople; panic spread across Europe, and it seemed as if the whole Christian Church was in danger. But the Papacy was on its guard and had managed to salvage a large number of ancient manuscripts from the pillaged East; in this way some of the finest treasures of human thought were saved from destruction by the Turks. The Pope was at that time living under very cramped conditions at the Vatican, as the Lateran was uninhabitable, but he readily took care of the books. This was the beginning of the Vatican Library, which has today become one of the most important literary and scientific sources. Its organization is without parallel in the whole world and it employs scholars of every race and tongue to continue the ceaseless work of classifying and annotating. Scarcely had the texts arrived than the scholars who were deciphering them became extremely interested in the literature they contained and, moreover, in classical philosophy and pagan architecture. The spirit of renaissance quickly caught fire and soon passed the bounds of Christian restraint. A great wave of the new artistic feeling swept over Rome. The popes were far too well trained to miss their opportunity and began to patronize the artists, encouraging the lively competitive spirit which sprang up. Almost immediately they realized the dangers of the new fashion and gave instructions to the scholars and artists concerned only to use this new knowledge about the past with discretion and for the good of Christianity. It was at this time, in the middle of the fifteenth century, that the first printed page appeared at Strasbourg; the wooden block used had been carved by Gutenberg. It is worth noting here that printing was invented to make copies of the Holy Scriptures more readily available. All these new discoveries and inventions, and the fall of the Byzantine Empire, marked the closing stages of the Middle Ages. Unfortunately some witnesses of these new events became impatient and scandalized. Luther let his hatred ripen into open revolt, leading many astray from the paths of Rome. To understand Rome is a divine grace. This gift is lost by jealousy, disobedience, ambition and foolhardiness. It is an evil day when one no longer listens to the voice of the Universal Father.

Sixtus IV, who founded the Sistine Chapel, wanted to keep the early basilica of St Peter's intact; he saw it as the embodiment of twelve centuries of the Church's glorious history. However, others preferred to symbolize this great past in a completely new building, designed in such a way as to bring out all the youth and vigour of the Church. The work started by Nicholas V was finished by Julius II, Leo X and Paul III; in the place of the old basilica, which they pulled down, arose the magnificent church that is still one of the wonders of the world. Our admiration must outweigh any regrets; who can fail to admire the extraordinary breadth of vision that led to such a work? Of truly Roman proportions, it is a worthy temple for the crowds of faithful believers which have been visiting it ever since.

The new St Peter's is quite different from the old, at least for the art historian. No longer do we find one great room, designed with the liturgy in mind; instead there is something planned on the colossal scale. Man here has used all his skill and daring to pay homage to God; by calculating thrust and balance, the contrast of straight lines and curves, the relationships of space to mass and the play of light, he produced the most convincing proof possible of the primacy of the Apostolic message. One must be a Christian to realize the full meaning of St Peter's. Even then the first impression when one enters may be disappointing, so perfect are its proportions. It is only when one gets to know it better that the full significance of its size is understood, a size that is suitable to its long history. Although the plan followed by Bramante, Michelangelo and Maderna necessitated the removal of most of the earlier buildings, St Peter's has always stood on the same site; besides, its name and its traditions have continued unchanged, so it may be considered as always having been the same church since it was first consecrated. People have gone there to pray during the whole of its long history.

What a wonderful thing it is that one can trace the succession from St Peter to Pius XII without a break! No other church can hold nearly such a big congregation as St Peter's, a fact worthy of the scale of the Sovereign Pontiff's ministry. In the same way one can say that the dome is on the same scale as the eternal city; the moment one can see its beautiful curve in the distance one can say: "Rome!" And in the shadow of the dome lies the Vatican, the hub of the Roman Church. In its rooms are the escutcheons of all the popes who had a hand in building it and who lived there; their history is closely linked with that of the western world and in it are recorded the many blessings and miracles wrought by the crucified Saviour.

The opening section of this introduction has tried to show what Rome means to the Church, what are some of its many attractions and its pride. It has tried, too, to show a little of what one cannot see at first glance. Devotees of Rome are always happy there, and when a person is full of such thoughts as we have described, how much he will enjoy going to see the great collections and museums of the city, the Belvedere and the Vatican, and what profit he will draw from them. Art books make it more and more possible for people to enjoy all these treasures at home, but they can never provide the equivalent of being present at one of the great ceremonies of the Church. He who can do so is indeed most fortunate. Every detail of them is planned, from the decorations to the procedure of the ritual. All the rules are traditional and they are applied to the particular ceremony by the masters of ceremonies, who organize every movement. All the hardships of a pilgrim are for the one purpose of the privilege of an audience with the Holy Father or the sight of him taking part in all the splendour of a papal function.

Each morning there is a steady procession through the major-domo's office, consisting of pilgrims begging the favour of an audience with the Pope. They approach timidly, hardly daring to ask, but everyone has the same wish: to see the Pope, kiss his hand and talk to him, or even just to be present when he celebrates Mass. Actually Pius XII insists on his Mass being private so that he can give full attention to the Holy Sacrifice and pray undisturbed; it is from his heartfelt contemplation at these times that he finds the answers to his many problems. He has so much work; but then he loves it, both his own and other people's. He always tries to avoid keeping prelates idle at his side; when he celebrates Mass in public, as for instance on the Thursday in Holy Week or at the Christmas Midnight Mass, they must always be in attendance. So on those days, when he has to give Communion to his Papal Family in the first case, and to the *Corps Diplomatique* in the second—and occasionally when he has to give children their first Communion—he is always to be found in the Capella Matilda or the Capella Paolina, a perfect example of a holy priest at the altar.

According to the number of those taking part, public audiences are held in various places; in the Vatican palace itself, in either the

Clementine, Ducal or Royal rooms, or in the room of the Benediction; above the portico of St Peter's; in the courts of S. Damaso or the Belvedere; or even in the basilica itself, a frequent practice in Holy Year. The Pope is carried to the audience on the *sedia*, accompanied by a large retinue; if it is being held in St Peter's he is enthroned before the high altar and then gives an address in seven or eight different languages. Millions have heard these talks; addressed in a fatherly way, they show to humanity how there is only one way to salvation and are touching appeals for justice, peace, courage and active faith. The cheers and applause show how much the present Pope is loved and respected. Happy are they who can gather round him and perhaps catch his eye; fortunate if they can keep his words in their hearts.

Twice Pius XII has gone outside the precincts of the Vatican for audiences. At the time of the bombing of the Tiburtina station near S. Lorenzo and again when the Via Appia near S. Giovanni in Laterano was bombed he hurriedly went to his diocesans to give help and comfort. His compassion and generous gifts helped to calm their fears. He prayed for the victims and tended the wounded, staining his white soutane with their blood. When he stretched out his arms to give his blessing a wave of horror swept over the crowd, for they thought he had been wounded. Rome will not forget those two tragic audiences. On June 5th, 1944, the whole of Rome somehow heard, despite the fact that there were no papers, no wireless and no transport, that Rome was to be liberated without any fighting; everyone went to the Vatican to thank Pius XII for the part he had played in having the city spared. The most sacred heritage of Christianity was saved and the Pope justly earned the title of "Saviour of Rome". On the tenth anniversary of this event the Rome city council came to renew their homage and thanks; the crowd has come many times for audience to St Peter's Square.

Special audiences are held in the rooms on the east and south sides of the second floor of the Vatican. At these, after a few private audiences, the Holy Father walks through the gathering, which consists of little groups, families and a few important people; as he goes he talks for a moment here and there, holds out his hand to be kissed and then gives his blessing. Often he gives out a rosary or a medal and the recipient takes it kneeling, happy as a child to have been given a memento that will become one of his dearest possessions. There is something very moving about the simplicity and generosity of this Pope, who moves dressed in white amidst these sumptuous surroundings. The tapestried walls, ceilings painted blue, red and deep green—the azure, gules and sinople of heraldry—with gold decorations on top are all reminders of the sovereigns who have ruled here before, each with his richly coloured enamelled coat-of-arms. Voices, footfalls, everything here is subdued and gives an air of respect and slight mystery. The memory of this moment will always be vivid—the wait, the moment he arrives and the sight of him; one knows then how deeply one loves him.

Some of these audiences occur on regular dates. On December 24th each year the Dean of the Sacred College of Cardinals reads out a Christmas address to the Holy Father, surrounded by the clergy of Rome; this is the preface to the Pope's broadcast Christmas Message, which is important both doctrinally and for summing up the contemporary trend of events. There is also a fixed date when the ambassadors of all nations come to pay the respects of their country to the Pope and take back his answer to their sovereigns. On January 21st is the Blessing of the Lambs of St Agnes; later the wool from their fleeces will be woven into palliums. On February 2nd after the Candlemas service the clergy of all the basilicas and national churches in Rome bring the Pope a decorated wax candle which they have blessed. Just before Lent all those who are going to preach during the coming month go to the Holy Father to receive his instructions. Other special audiences are rather more solemn occasions still; such as when the Pope has to speak to monks or nuns on the anniversary of their general Chapter, or to large groups of representatives varying from teachers to soldiers, from industrialists to athletes. These talks make a deep impression on their hearers; above all, they are struck by the way that the Pope knows so much about everyone's professions. Once, when Pius XII was talking to a group of Radiologists, in April 1954, he said: "Nothing which is of any importance to the increase of knowledge and the happiness of humanity is uninteresting to Us." How moving it is to read in his fine handwriting his blessing on the English doctors:

How exalted, how worthy of all honour is the *one* character of your profession
The doctor has been appointed by God Himself) *(cfr. Ecli. 38, 1)* to minister to the needs of suffering
humanity. He who created that fever - consumed or mangled frame, now in
your hands, who loves it with an eternal love, confides to you the ennobling
charge of restoring it to health. You will bring to the sick - room and the operati°
table something of the charity of God, of the love and tenderness of Christ,
the Master Physician of soul and body.

That the blessing of the King of Kings may descend *g* upon you and
your work and
all your dear ones and your beloved country and remain forever, is the wish
and prayer that rise from Our affectionate heart.

But the supreme moment is when one receives a folded paper sealed with the yellow-and-white stamp of the Papal Antechamber, telling one that His Holiness will graciously grant a private audience at such-and-such a time. The Cardinals of the Curia have theirs on fixed dates, depending upon whether they are members of a congregation, a

30

tribunal or an office; hence the name *de Tabella* for these audiences, and also for the ambassadors' audience. Bishops must come and give an account of their ministry to the Sovereign Pontiff every three or five years, depending on their distance from Rome; their journey is called *ad limina Apostolorum*—"towards the threshold, the tomb of the Apostles". They put in a request for an audience the moment they arrive in Rome, as do all who wish to negotiate with the Sovereign Pontiff direct.

A private audience must surely be one of the greatest experiences in the life of any Roman Catholic. A great many doors have to be opened and many rooms crossed before you finally arrive. First you are conducted by Swiss Guards, then by *sediari* in livery of cerise damask, then by officers of the Palatine Guard wearing the kepi with a chin-strap. Next come guards drawn from the nobility who are dressed in red, followed by chamberlains of honour in black coats with blue collars. Finally, in soutanes and long purple mantles with crimson linings, come the clerical chamberlains accompanied by the noble who is not on guard and who is bareheaded; with them are other chamberlains with gold-embroidered red collars on their black capes and swords by their sides. This last group takes you right up to the threshold of the private library; for the last four centuries this has been the office of the Pope. A bell announces the end of the previous audience, the confidential chamberlain opens the door and, setting the example, genuflects on the doorstep; one step forward—the Pope is seen as in a vision sitting at his desk—another genuflexion; His Holiness looks welcomingly at you and you hurry towards him, dropping on your knees at his feet in filial piety and respect to take his outstretched hand. It is a very thrilling moment even for a cardinal; there you are alone before the Most Holy and Blessed Vicar of Christ, who is guided by the Holy Spirit; there is the Sovereign and Universal Father listening to all that you have to say, making observations and comparisons, thinking for a time, foreseeing difficulties, taking things into account. He is a kind of divine providence, working for the good of individual people and whole nations. It is extremely hard work for him; there must hardly be a day without some problem arising, hardly a night without some worry. But there he carries on at his desk like his predecessors, Pius XI, Benedict XV and St Pius X, like Leo XIII and Pius IX.

*
* *

The extraordinary continuity and immutability of the Church is pictured in the record of the Popes of the last hundred years, made possible by the invention of photography, collotype and, later, photogravure in the reign of Pius IX. Before, there were some portraits and engravings of the popes, but now there are so many photographs that their faces have become as familiar to all Catholics as those of members of their own families. Moreover, they are always dressed the same and are seen surrounded by the same officials and objects in the Vatican, or taking part in the same sacred rituals, or sitting at the same desk working for humanity.

His Holiness Pius XII is the living embodiment of this last century of papal history. Perhaps never before has there been a pope who was better prepared for this supreme office and who served it so faithfully and untiringly. Eugenio Pacelli was born on March 2nd, 1876, two years before the death of Pius IX; his family bore the affairs of Rome very close to its heart. He had loved Rome and the Vatican from his earliest years and had often gone to see the Pope at St Peter's, as his family lived just on the other side of the Tiber. Leo XIII was Pope while he was at school and at seminary and also provided the perfect example for him while he was a young priest. The young Pacelli had a quick brain and an unusually good memory; he loved work and had a particular liking for philology; his holidays were spent in learning languages. His faith and piety and complete lack of fear brought him the admiration of his fellow students, although there was of course to some extent a feeling of rivalry. His sense of vocation showed that above all these exceptional qualities he had the one that was essential, a deep love of God. He was ordained priest in 1899; soon he became Professor of Canon Law at the papal school of St Apollinarius, at which a short time before he had been a pupil; by then it had moved to the Lateran. His ministry was at the Chiesa Nuova and, apart from preaching, hearing confessions and teaching the catechism, he spent most of his leisure hours there. However, it was at the Vatican that his fate was to lie. He was chosen by the Secretariat of State as the Pope's *Minutante*; this office involves editing and correcting the Pope's speeches and minutes. He took up the appointment with some regret, for he thought he had been cut out to be a professor. But God had more important work for him. St Pius X was Pope in the later years of his priesthood and at the Vatican Dom Eugenio Pacelli met all those in the papal court. He became the disciple of Cardinals Rampolla and Merry del Val, and also of Mgr della Chiesa and Mgr Gasparri. He was particularly closely connected with Mgr Gasparri, as he became his secretary, and his work involved drawing up the documents concerning France after the Separation of Church and State and the recasting of the Canon Law. His opinions found favour and he was rapidly moved up through the various grades in the Secretariat of State; at the death of St Pius X he was the Pro-Secretary of State. Cardinal della Chiesa became Benedict XV and it was during this time that Mgr Pacelli became a bishop. Certain of his capabilities, the Pope sent him as Nuncio to Bavaria; after the Concordat with this country there came the Concordat with Prussia, while also at this time the difficult Roman Question, which was later to be settled by the Conciliation with Italy, was being discussed. Pius XI chose him for his Cardinal Secretary of State and sent him as his representative on voyages all round the world; he inspired trust and admiration in all he met and was a shining example of all that the Papacy stands for. The great successes of the Catholic Church in the world today are without doubt due to his excellent work. It must be agreed that no one could have been more qualified to become Pope.

Pius XI has been named Pope of the "Peace of Christ in the Kingdom of Christ"; he gave up his life for that peace. On February 10th, 1939, he died and the world went into mourning. On the evening of March 1st the sixty-two Cardinals shut themselves in Conclave at the Vatican. On the morning of March 2nd they went to Mass in the Sistine Chapel and then took a first vote for the new Pope; each one as he put his ballot paper into the chalice made a solemn vow: "I call Christ Our Saviour, who will be my judge, to witness that I elect the man whom I consider God wills should be elected." People thought at the time that by the second vote Cardinal Pacelli would certainly be elected. A little after midday, however, black smoke was still coming from the special chimney in the Sistine Chapel; it came from burning ballot papers mixed with damp straw and showed that another vote had been necessary. In the evening, just before half-past five, white smoke coming from the chimney showed that a single day of Conclave had been enough. The news quickly spread across Rome; as night fell the crowd collected in St Peter's Square while all the time the ritual was going on inside the Vatican; first, the acceptance of the new Pope, then the choice of his name, dressing him in the white robe, his investiture, and finally the procession of cardinals to pay him homage. Meanwhile, the Cardinal Dean of the Deacons Caccia Dominioni came out into the central loggia of the Basilica and proclaimed: "I bring you news of great joy, we have a Pope." When he named Eugenio Pacelli cheers rang out. He went on to say that the new Pope had been elected on his birthday and that his name would be Pius. There came the *Te Deum*, followed by the first *urbi et orbi* Blessing; this blessing is given to the city of Rome and the whole world and the words rang out over a kneeling crowd. Immediately afterwards everyone stood up and acclaimed the new Pope. Then came one of the most moving parts of the ceremony, the prayer *Oremus pro Pontifice nostro Pio*, which is always sung in the presence of the Pope himself.

Pius IX had been crowned on June 21st, 1846, and according to tradition the ceremony had taken place in the outside loggia of St

34

Peter's. Owing to various reasons Leo XIII had received the tiara in the Sistine Chapel and St Pius X, Benedict XV and Pius XI in the inside loggia of the Basilica. When Pius XII was crowned on March 12th, 1939, there was nothing to stop the full ceremonial which had not been seen for a whole century, as the Lateran Treaty had just been signed. It was one of the most magnificent coronations that Rome has ever seen. There were more clergy than usual and the crowd was vast. Apart from special delegates from nearly all the nations of the world, including non-Catholic nations, there were also kings, queens and princes. St Peter's had been decorated with red hangings and thousands of lights in chandeliers. It was a magnificent procession that moved down from the Vatican into the body of the church. One could hardly imagine any man being surrounded with more glorious pomp and ceremony; yet at the same time there were many reminders of humility for the "Servant of the servants of God". In front of him was carried a *ferula*, the threatening rod that is used in the penitentiary, and also a gilded cane surmounted by a piece of burning tow. As the flames went up from it, it was a clear reminder of the transience of this world's glories; *sic transit*. There were many invocations and litanies and to each the answer was "Help him". As Pius XII started celebrating his first Papal Mass and reached the *Mea culpa* of the Confiteor he struck himself on the chest. It was only after this long preparation that he could face the supreme test of being crowned without any risk of pride.

After the ceremony the procession formed up again inside the Basilica and, to the sound of peels of bells and the Pontifical Hymn, moved out into the loggia. The waiting crowd in the piazza outside saw the red-uniformed vexillifer come out into the daylight bearing the standard of the Holy Roman Church. This standard is a relic of the Crusades. When Pius XII appeared, the noise was deafening and the military fanfares were hardly audible. However, the silence when Cardinal Caccia placed the triple crown on the Sovereign Pontiff's head was even more impressive. This triple crown has a threefold meaning;

35

it is the symbol of the Pope's doctrinal, sacramental and pastoral authority passed down to him from Jesus Christ, Prophet, Priest and Pastor. It is thus a sign of the all-inclusive power of the Pope and the primacy of St Peter. After this, Pius XII rose and, as the crowd went down on its knees, flags were dipped and the troops presented arms, he called upon his great new power and gave out his Papal Blessing to the world. The Universal Father was to see his Church gathered together at his feet on many occasions after this. A similar ceremony takes place at midday on Easter Day and whenever large groups of pilgrims or representatives come to Rome, and each time the Pope addresses them and gives them his Blessing.

The pageantry of those glorious days did not stop at nightfall. Flood-lights were turned on and the cross on the top of the dome of St Peter's shone out against the star-filled Roman night. It was a sight to conjure up the memory of the past and the whole course of history seemed to unfold around this man of God. Sent to bring light and peace into the world, each successor of St Peter knows that his office is undying and that there is nothing to fear. Although his own work will never be completed he knows that God will see that it is continued. What is past for us was to the people of a short time ago the future, and even as the promise of those years was faithfully fulfilled, so the Church can be confident of its future today. Rome, city of souls, has travelled a long way up to the present time and its endurance and achievements in the past encourage us to strike out into the future. On the evening of November 1st, 1950, a new arrangement was started at the Vatican. A window was kept illuminated and at midnight and 6 a.m., times when the Holy Father could not normally grant audience, he showed himself to the pilgrims who waited below. What a wonderful sight it was, that huge crowd twice a day on their knees receiving the Apostolic Blessing! What better display could there possibly be of fatherly affection?

After the Pope is crowned he must be enthroned and his first move is to take possession of his Papal and Pontifical See at S. Salvatoris in the Lateran. This ceremony is called the *Possesso*. The procession forms up in the Patriarchal Palace. At the entrance of the Basilica the keys are given to the Bishop of Rome, Patriarch of the West, who goes to his throne in the cathedral. From that position he first pays homage to the Sacred Heads, St Peter and St Paul, and afterwards goes to celebrate Mass at the wooden altar. This altar encloses the Eucharistic Table used by St Peter. It was reserved for the use of the Pope by St Sylvester in 327, when he consecrated this very holy church as *Mater et Caput*—Mother and Head of all the churches in Rome and the rest of the world. Afterwards, the *urbe et orbi* Blessing is given from the loggia of S. Giovanni in Laterano. The façade of this church was built by Galilei in 1735 and the balcony is perfectly designed to form the focal point of this magnificent ceremony.

The *Possesso* of Pius XII took place on Ascension Day, May 18th, 1939. In 1846 the whole cavalcade of the Roman court had turned out for the last time to honour Pius IX, but the beauty of those wonderful horses and carriages has now disappeared. The crowd did not take as much interest in the ceremony then as it does nowadays; people who were present still enthusiastically describe the sight that met the eyes of Pius XII. The huge space between the Lateran and S. Croce was completely covered with people. Both papal and Italian troops had come to honour him, and their flags and brightly coloured uniforms made a stirring sight. It seemed as if the fanfares and *vivats* would never come to an end. Each year on the anniversary of the Crowning the Diocesan Bishops of Rome meet at the Lateran for a solemn *Te Deum*. The Cardinal Archpriest Aloisi-Masella presides, surrounded by the Venerable Chapter.

The Crowning and the *Possesso* are the highest honours accorded to the new Pontiff; now the ceaseless obligations of the Pontificate begin. No longer will the Church centre its worship on him but on God and the saints; henceforth his time will not be his own, for the Pope can never be completely free of commitments.

Most of the great ceremonies in Rome centre round the ritual of the Papal Mass, the Mass which the Pope intones himself. He did this at the Crowning and at the *Possesso* in the Lateran; in future he will have to do it at Canonizations and at proclamations of Dogma, which either precede the Mass or are included in it. The Papal Mass by itself, as on Easter Day, is quite magnificent. At the moment of the consecration of the Bread and Wine as the Body and Blood of Christ, and when the Pope lifts them at the Elevation and presents them to the four points of the compass, a believer trembles with emotion. He sees in the celebration of the Eucharist the Saviour destroyed for the salvation of the world and it is like a vision of the sacrifice on Sinai. The non-believer can scarcely fail to be filled with admiration and respect at the sight, and perhaps his opinion of the Church may reach its highest point. He will regard it as finer than the most magnificent opera he can ever see, and think that there is nothing in the world that can compare with it. In this great ceremony all that is noble on earth is combined to pay homage to God. Every artifice is used to make the building, the robes, the music and the lighting more beautiful. The congregation represents the whole of humanity: the *Corps Diplomatique*, the nations of the world; the army, honour and courage; the clergy, the Holiness of the Church. And in those sacred and poetic words which the Sovereign Pontiff pronounces, as the man nearest to God, is heard the earth's suppliant prayer to the Almighty. Nothing could be more majestic and beautiful.

A little later the Sacred Host and the Chalice are taken from the altar to the throne for the Communion of the Holy Father. His presence, his obvious emotion and his inner contemplation make it quite clear that he lets nothing of what is going on around him interfere with his communion with Christ. Onlookers murmur "What great faith", and think how lucky they are to be there. Who can tell what miracles take place within the souls of men during these holy ceremonies?

One of the rites of the Papal Mass that attracts most attention is the intoning of the Epistle and the Gospel in Greek. A subdeacon, a deacon and the Schola of the Greek college are there and their many-coloured robes and the strangely evocative cadence of the Eastern melodies add greatly to the Roman Catholic liturgy. It is striking proof of the affinity between the Western and Eastern Churches despite the great difference in their liturgies, for the liturgy of Rome is very different from that of the Byzantines, or the Syriacs; or from those of the Maronites, the Chaldeans, the Armenians or the Copts. In the Holy Year of 1950 proof was given of this unity when His Beatitude Maxim IV Saïgh, Patriarch of Antioch of the Melchites, was invited to Rome. He was asked to celebrate Mass with fourteen of his bishops in the Basilica of St Peter's, in the presence of the Sovereign Pontiff. As he did so a great desire for unity was felt round the tomb of the Prince of Apostles. In the heartfelt longing of the great congregation of pilgrims who had come from all over the world, Christ's prayer after the Last Supper was re-offered. Just as He had asked Peter and His disciples to be one even as He and His Father were One, so this great gathering prayed for the union of all the churches in the world under one supreme authority.

The proclamation of a dogma is one of the rarest events in the history of the Church. The Immaculate Conception of the Virgin Mary was proclaimed on December 8th, 1854, and the memorable festivities, which were centred round Pius IX on that occasion, were revived in the centenary Marian Year of 1954. The dogma of the Papal Infallibility, July 18th, 1870, was the last act of the Vatican Council before it was interrupted by the Franco-Prussian War. The signal privilege of adding another

39

adornment to the Virgin's diadem was reserved for His Holiness Pius XII. He completed the dogma of her Immaculate Conception with that of her glorious Assumption to the sky. He was supported unanimously by the entire Catholic world. The Proclamation was the culminating point of the Jubilee Year, 1950, and the crowd which gathered was the largest that had ever been seen at Rome. It filled both the Basilica of St Peter's and the whole piazza outside. There were eight hundred bishops around the Holy Father on that unique All Saints' Day morning. The sky, which at first had been overclouded, cleared to such a limpid blue that it amazed everybody there, and into it rose the pale crescent of the moon. The most impressive moment was not the intoning of the litany by Cardinal Tisserant, the Dean of the Sacred College, nor the reading by the Pope of the infallible opening words of the dogma: *"Definimus, decretamus et confirmamus"*, but the deep moment of silence between the two commands of the cardinal deacons, *"Orate"* and *"Levate"*, the meditation of a million people praying, on their knees with the Holy Father. God was there, earth and heaven were one.

It was the same at the Canonization of St Pius X. The Papal Mass which followed was a magnificent scene; the bishops sat on the green draped tiers of seats which had been prepared for them in the apse, as if they were at an oecumenical council. According to custom the Pope's throne was placed at the foot of the Throne of St Peter at the end of a long vista of archbishops and bishops. In front of them, lower down, were the high benches of the cardinals. This fabulous scene can only be recalled by photographs like those in this book.

The world had gathered together, the many-coloured crowd of pilgrims rang with the sound of every language; Rome appeared in her true light as the capital of Christianity devoted to Mary. Rome itself is a Marian city. It does not take long to see that. At the cross-roads, the corners of the houses are often adorned with a relief set into the wall representing the Madonna whom baroque art has framed in clouds and stucco angels. Sometimes she has become the protectress of a quarter;

then she is surrounded with flowers, and photographs of the absent are entrusted to her, especially those of young men away on military service. With a lamp burning in front of her she is enthroned above shop counters or at the back of hotel rooms, like a family portrait. The Holy Virgin is an ancestress, she is the mother of all men just as much in a poor shop or a streamlined bar as at the Vatican or in religious communities: Mary, the peace, the joy, the salvation of the world, mother of Divine Love, through whom Christ became our brother. It is she who today rules the hour of the evening with the ringing of the Angelus, the *Ave Maria*. It varies by a quarter of an hour a fortnight, following the twilight and announcing in summer the cold north wind, the *tramontana*. All Christians know this telegraphic language of the Church: for centuries they have heard these bells. Three times a day they retell the Annunciation to Mary of the redemption of the world. Rome was clearly revealed as the city of Mary in May 1947, when the Mayor, Rebecchini, stood before the Madonna in the Capitoline Basilica of Aracoeli and solemnly consecrated the town to her Immaculate Heart. It was obvious too on the evening of December 8th, 1949, when in spiritual preparation for the Holy Year, the Roman people gave an ecstatic triumph to the painting of the Madonna venerated as "Their Salvation". This painting, the "*Salus Populi Romani*", is traditionally attributed to St Luke himself. It was carried in procession from Santa Maria Maggiore to St Peter's where Pius XII came to greet it. Again, on December 8th, 1953, Rome was seen as the city of Mary when the Pope opened the special Jubilee Year, with spiritual favours extended to all the sanctuaries of Our Lady throughout the world. His Holiness Pius XII crossed Rome in an official procession to kneel in the Piazza di Spagna before a statue of the Immaculate Conception consecrated by Pius IX one hundred years before. Then he continued towards the basilica on the Esquiline hill, where he read the wonderful prayer which he had composed for this Marian Year. And every day of 1954 this devotion to Mary could be seen in the Borghese chapel of Santa Maria Maggiore, the centre of continual prayer. It was

41

here that the splendours of the Canonization of St Pius X were prolonged throughout the octave by popular devotion.

St Pius X was beatified on June 3rd, 1951, according to the usual ritual. The decree was read by a canon of St Peter's, before the pontifical Mass was celebrated at the apsidal altar by a cardinal. In the evening, the Holy Father came down to worship the *Beato* and his remains which were exposed in a shrine. This time also there were crowds of pilgrims in the piazza, and before the Blessing of the Holy Sacrament Pius XII uttered an important and magnificent panegyric. The Canonization was the most solemn occasion in 1954. On the evening of May 29th the spectacle was the same as on the morning of All Saints' Day, 1950; an immense crowd, the official stands of the *Corps Diplomatique*, Ambassadors, Knights of the Holy Sepulchre and of Malta; a wonderful procession; and lastly the Holy Father. He received a tremendous ovation from the crowd who were full of joy at seeing his smile again and his affectionate gestures. In a sonorous voice, he spoke the oration and the declaration of infallibility, *ex cathedra*, from his chair as Doctor of the Universal Church. The whole crowd, and everyone throughout the world who was listening in, believed with him that at that moment his predecessor Pius X had become a saint. Then he gave a masterly discourse on his motto: "Everything leads to unity in Christ".

Sunday morning, May 30th, Cardinal Tisserant, Dean of the Sacred College, had the rare honour of singing the Mass of Canonization at the papal altar, in front of which the shrine of Pius X was exposed. Surrounded by bishops, the Holy Father presided on his throne in mitre and papal mantle. This is known as a Papal Chapel to distinguish it from a Mass which is actually said by the Pope. The traditional and gracious offerings of tapers and birds were presented at the throne. The wonderful light and the beauty of the music added to the fervour of the prayer. Afterwards, the Benediction *urbi et orbi* held the crowd on the piazza for a few moments longer and then the waves of people disappeared from the Holy City of the Vatican. The liturgical rites were over. In the afternoon, there was a popular triumph to conduct Pius X in procession across Rome to Santa Maria Maggiore. It was an unforgettable sight; the whole capital lined the streets to pay a spontaneous homage of devotion to this symbol of the sanctifying influence of the Papacy. Streets, bridges, squares, the whole town was truly God's largest temple. Light and shadow played on the silver face of the dead man in the shrine so that for a moment he seemed to be alive again. The cardinals were waiting at the door of Santa Maria Maggiore and made a purple ring around this exemplar of the Christian life whose lessons they would carry across the world.

Since the first jubilee instituted by Boniface VIII in A.D. 1300, the faithful have gathered in Rome to obtain the great indulgence twenty-five times. This indulgence the Church grants four times a century in her concern for the salvation of people's souls. But never has any pope seen such an amazing sight as that continually seen by Pius XII during 1950. It was an exceptional Holy Year, which he called "the year of the great return and the great pardon". These words sum up the whole purpose and result of the Jubilee. In 1950 Christians were asked to return to a more practical and lively faith, which would lead them to repentance and a better life. For it is the spirit of repentance that leads to true contribution and the firm resolve to turn to a more holy life because it is more pleasing to God. That was the great return. Only by such resolutions are souls ready to receive the great pardon. By coming to Rome they recognize that here only is the doorway to salvation, that here is the true fatherland of all Catholics and the home of the Vicar of Christ, the visible sign of the

Kingdom of God in the world. At Rome the pilgrim fulfils his obligations. Pius XII reduced these to one visit to each of the four great basilicas which form the spiritual square of the Roman faith.

On June 2nd, 1948, the feast-day of his saint, St Eugene, Pius XII announced the Jubilee. On May 26th, 1949, he signed the Bill of Indiction. On July 12th he defined the special intentions for the year. On December 24th he proceeded solemnly, with all the traditional and symbolic rites, to the opening of the Holy Door of St Peter's. At the same time his Legates *a latere*, that is to say the Legates through whom he is present, opened the Holy Doors of San Giovanni in Laterano, San Paolo fuori le Mura and Santa Maria Maggiore. Holding a lighted taper, the Pope struck the wall three times with a precious hammer, asking that "he might open the door of holiness, to enter the house of the Lord and have Him with us". Pius XI had bricked up the wall and blessed it after the last time it was opened in 1933. The wall fell back in one piece and the Pope went through first, holding a cross. After him came that endless procession which for a whole year fell on their knees to kiss the threshold in a spirit of humility and penitence and to seek remission of the sufferings incurred by their errors and faults.

The joy at the opening of the door was only matched by the sadness when it was closed up again. Pilgrims wept, and there was widespread grief, particularly amongst those who had witnessed the fervour of people passing through this doorway of grace. The Church, which can bind and loose, resumed her extreme readiness to grant salvation. Perhaps people had not profited sufficiently from it at Rome; so, like a good mother, the Church now extended her favours to the Universal Church, who continued the Jubilee for another year throughout the world. Surrounded by the same solemn pomp on December 24th, 1950, Pius XII, kneeling, blessed the bricks, lime and sand. With a silver-gilt trowel he spread mortar on the threshold and laid one gilded and two silvered bricks in place, asking God to guard the sanctuary where so many souls had found the benefits of grace.

44

During the Holy Year pilgrims flocked to Rome. The Central Committee, under its President Mgr Valerio Valeri, since created Cardinal, carried out a tremendous work of charity and organization. The Holy Father himself made many Jubilee visits. At St Peter's all the clergy of Rome formed his retinue. In August he visited the other three basilicas, not from the Vatican but from his summer palace at Castelgandolfo. This led the press to speak of the "Pilgrim of Castelgandolfo". The Pope's activity during the twelve months was prodigious; there were numbers of audiences and ceremonies which necessitated the continual preparation of addresses. The *Pastor Angelicus*, the shepherd, never rested. As if he were an angel sent by God, he listened incessantly to the calls of his flock, knowing how often they are led astray.

The town of Rome is also his concern. It expands rapidly and continually needs new churches in the new districts. These lack the long tradition of Roman piety and the inhabitants are in grave danger of losing the habit of religious observance. To show his concern and to bless the work of the Vicariate, His Holiness consecrated the altar of the Church of St Eugene, which had been built by the Christian world as homage to the Pope in his sacerdotal and episcopal Jubilee Year. The soil of Rome has produced many churches, but at certain times it seems to rest like a field which has just yielded a rich harvest. Unusual circumstances have prolonged these winters, while others have encouraged an abundant spring as at the present time, when the population of one suburb has increased by a million inhabitants over the last thirty years. St Sylvester and Constantine brought about the first spring, whose fruits can still be seen today. Can one look forward to new heights of glory like the centuries of the Renaissance or the Roman Baroque, that most Catholic of styles? Divine blessing increases temples, as it has increased the generations of men, and it has always favoured this patriarchal town of the Christian world. Modern artists have at their disposal so many new materials, more varied than ever before and easier to use. It is to be hoped

45

that they will not be led astray but will prepare the way for a great epoch of Christian art.

The Palazzo de Carolis has been the scene of splendid occasions. Here Cardinal de Bernis, the ambassador of Louis XV, gave his lavish entertainments; and here on December 28th, 1828, René de Chateaubriand, Charles X's representative to Leo XII, sat down to write after a large reception: "We have had all the Cardinals! All Europe was here!" On January 15th, 1953, Count Vladimir d'Ormesson could write from the Villa Bonaparte, the French Embassy to the Holy See since 1951: "The whole world has been here!" How true this was. The vast crowd, which had come to congratulate the cardinals Feltin and Grente after their "creation" as cardinals, had at last left the Villa Bonaparte. There is always a "Ricevimento", a solemn reception, after great papal ceremonies and many ambassadors could have said the same on similar occasions. They make the beneficent influence of Catholic Rome tangible. Eminent people from the four corners of the world had met that morning in St Peter's and understood more fully the ties that bound them to the same Father and their universal redemption by Christ; the sight of the Holy Father had taken all their attention. Later, in the evening, they recognized one another, they rubbed shoulders, and though separated by nationality they felt themselves sons of a common fatherland. No doubt each of them had his national church, like St Thomas of Canterbury, St Suzanna, St Andrew of Scotland, or St Louis of the French whose guests they were; but such divisions were on that occasion no more than different rooms of one family home.

The two great public consistories of February 1946 and January 1953 have brought about this fusion in the Sacred College of Cardinals. Then Pope Pius XII chose his prelates from many distant lands which had never been represented before in the Church's Senate. The chosen candidates were invited to Rome by the State Secretariat. There they received the purple biretta at a secret, or at least semi-public, consistory, and a few days later the cardinal's hat was bestowed at a solemn ceremony. The hats are adorned with five rows of *fiocchi*, the fifteen red tassels which will henceforth be emblazoned on their armorial bearings. In 1946 unaccustomed splendour transformed the nave of St Peter's into an immense consistorial hall to mark the end of the sufferings of war and the renewal of the living forces of peace. In 1953 there was a slight shadow of austerity, but it could not dim the ceremonial majesty of the bestowal of the scarlet hat.

On his return to Paris, Cardinal Feltin described his great experiences from his throne in Notre Dame: "The chief impression that I have brought back with me is that from now on, as a cardinal of the Holy Church, I must work in the closest harmony with the Supreme Pontiff to strengthen and develop faith and loyalty to the Church in people's souls, and this must be done in a spirit of peace." He went on to define the office of cardinal and to explain the venerable and traditional splendour of the purple and the princely honours accorded to the order. Then he said: "The cardinals are the continuation of the *presbyterium*, the assembly of priests and deacons which ever since the early days of the Church always surrounded the Bishop of Rome, the supreme Head of Christianity. For a long time these counsellors lived in Rome, today only a few of them, called the Cardinals of the Curia, stay near the Pope; most of the others are bishops as well with a pastoral charge. They are men of every nation, of every language, of every colour and race, scattered over the world. This spreading of the Sacred College across the world fulfils a double need. The Pope wishes to be present everywhere in the person of his permanent delegates, the cardinals. . . . On the other hand all Christian peoples wish to be represented at the Holy See by a cardinal who is regarded as the official delegate for bringing information and objective decisions about their hopes and aspirations before the Papacy.

47

Thus the Holy Father by means of this pastoral order can act in full knowledge and take necessary measures in a perpetually changing world."

Seen from every point of view, Rome is always age-old, always eternal.

It is impossible to say everything about Rome, or even to say enough. One would like to say everything possible about His Holiness, Pius XII. The world regards him with love, almost with a kind of amazement, for in his character he combines all the different merits of the papal office. His life too has been so superabundant in good deeds that many of them would have been sufficient on their own to add glory to the Pontificate.

I hope that these pages will show the abundant vitality of the Church at Rome; her monuments are her adornment, they bear witness to her immortal soul which one must look for there. "No other city can be so beautiful", wrote Louis Veuillot. "No other sky, nor monuments, nor works of art, were they exactly the same, could in other surroundings have the same effect. Rome has an atmosphere all its own. One breathes there the history that God has written, and its lessons are applicable to each one of us. There, one has thoughts that could arise in no other place."

PIERRE PFISTER

48

I. THE SISTINE CHAPEL AND THE VATICAN
SEEN FROM THE TOP OF THE DOME

2. PLACE SAINT - PIERRE.
   SAINT PETER'S SQUARE.

3. COLONNADE DU BERNIN.
   BERNIN'S COLONNADE.

(Au verso, overleaf)

4. ILLUMINATIONS,
   8 DÉCEMBRE 1953.

   FLOODLIGHTING,
   DECEMBER 8, 1953.

5.
FAÇADE DE
SAINT-PIERRE.
LOGGIA DES
BÉNÉDICTIONS.

THE FAÇADE OF
SAINT PETER'S.
THE LOGGIA OF
BLESSINGS.

6.
ENVOLÉE DE
LA COUPOLE.

THE INSIDE OF
THE DOME.

UNE FENÊTRE BRILLE DANS LA NUIT.
A WINDOW SHINES IN THE NIGHT.

8. LE CHRIST-RÉDEMPTEUR BÉNIT SANS FIN.
CHRIST THE REDEEMER UNCEASINGLY BESTOWS HIS BLESSINGS.

PIUS IX

LEO XIII

BENEDICTUS

PIUS XI

9. UN SIÈCLE DE PAPAUTÉ.
THE POPES OF THE LAST CENTURY.

S. PIUS X

PIUS XII

II. A MUNICH EN 1917.
VOICI LE PAIN DU PÈRE.

IN MUNICH IN 1917.
HERE IS THE FATHER'S BREAD.

12. A BUENOS AYRES EN 1936.
VOICI LE PAIN DES ANGES.

IN BUENOS AYRES IN 1936.
HERE IS THE ANGELS' BREAD.

13. A LOURDES EN 1935.
AT LOURDES IN 1935.

14. PARIS-LISIEUX. JUILLET 1937.
PARIS - LISIEUX. JULY 1937.

15. ARRIVÉE AU CONCLAVE
ARRIVAL AT THE CONCLAVE.

16. LES SCELLÉS A LA
PORTE DU CONCLAVE.
16. THE SEALS AFFIXED ON
THE DOOR OF THE CONCLAVE.

18. A LA SIXTINE APRÈS L'ÉLECTION.
IN THE SISTINE CHAPEL AFTER HIS ELECTION.

19. OBÉDIENCE DES CARDINAUX
DUTIFUL SUBMISSION OF THE CARDINALS

20. COURONNEMENT.
12 MARS 1939.
CROWNING.
MARCH 12, 1939.

21. GROTTES VATICANES.
L'AUTEL "AD CAPUT".
THE GROTTOES OF THE VATICAN.
THE «AD CAPUT» ALTAR.

22. TE DEUM ANNIVERSAIRE
A SAINT-JEAN DE LATRAN.
ANNIVERSARY « TE DEUM »
AT THE LATERAN CHURCH.

23. MESSE PRIVÉE DU SAINT PÈRE.
THE HOLY FATHER'S PRIVATE MASS.

24. COMMUNION.
COMMUNION.

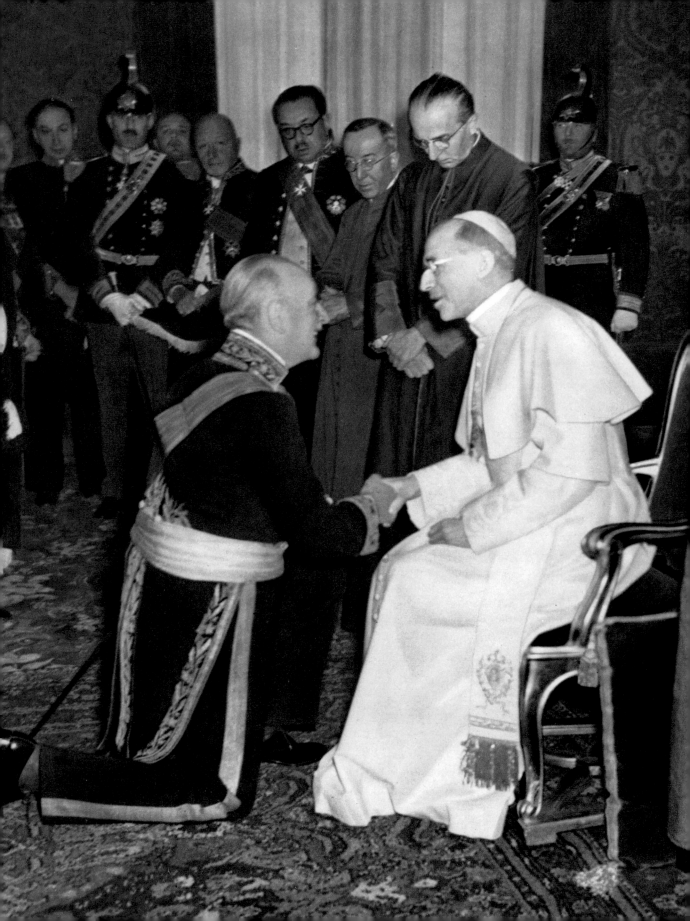

30. AUDIENCE PRINCIÈRE.
AUDIENCE OF PRINCES.

. AUDIENCE SOLENNELLE.
STATE AUDIENCE.

32. RELIGIEUSES.
NUNS.

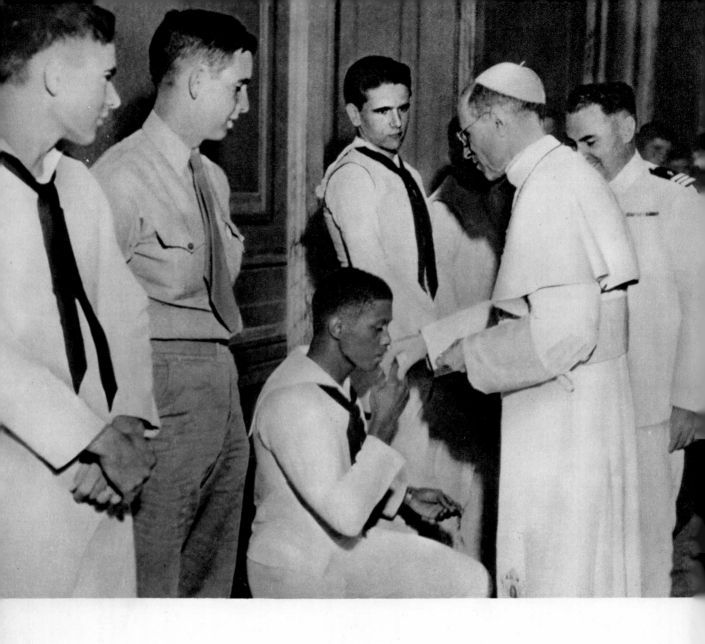

33. AUDIENCE MILITAIRE.
AUDIENCE OF AMERICAN SAILORS.

34. AUDIENCE POPULAIRE.
AUDIENCE OF THE COMMON PEOPL

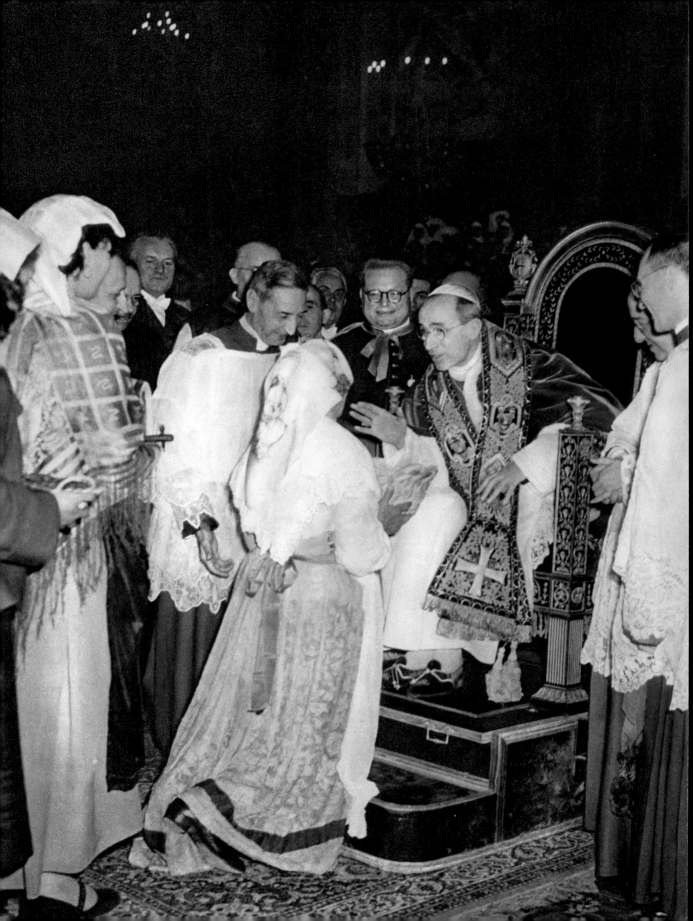

AUDIENCE EXOTIQUE.
EXOTIC AUDIENCE.

36. PETITS CHANTEURS.
LITTLE SINGERS.

37. LE ROYAUME DES
CIEUX EST A QUI
LEUR RESSEMBLE.

« FOR THE KINGDOM
OF HEAVEN IS FOR
SUCH ».

39. BÉATIFICATION.
BEATIFICATION.

38. LA PRIÈRE DU SAINT PÈRE.
THE HOLY FATHER'S PRAYER.

. LA CHÂSSE DE S. PIE X A L'AUTEL PAPAL.
THF SHRINE OF SAINT PIUS X AT THE PAPAL ALTAR.

. TRIDUUM DE S. PIE X A SAINTE-MARIE MAJEURE.
TRIDUUM FOR SAINT PIUS X AT S. MARIA MAGGIORE'S.

(Au verso, overleaf)
45. LE « POSSESSO » A SAINT-JEAN DE LATRAN.
THE « POSSESSO » AT SAINT JOHN LATERAN'S CHURCH.

(*Au recto, right-hand page*)

46. BÉNÉDICTION PAPALE DE LA LOGGIA DU LATRAN.
PAPAL BLESSING FROM THE LOGGIA OF THE LATERAN CHURCH.

47. OUVERTURE DE LA PORTE SAIN
OPENING THE HOLY DOO

48. LA PORTE OUVERTE.
THE DOOR ONCE OPENED.

49. LA PORTE SAINTE DU LATRAN.
THE HOLY DOOR OF THE LATERAN CHURCH.

50. LE CARDINAL LÉGAT MICARA AU LATRAN.
CARDINAL LEGATE MICARA AT THE LATERAN CHURCH.

51. VISITE JUBILAIRE A SAINT-JEAN DE LATRAN.
JUBILEE VISIT TO SAINT JOHN LATERAN'S CHURCH.

52.
VISITE JUBILAIRE
A SAINT-PAUL.
JUBILEE VISIT TO
SAINT PAUL'S

53.
A SAINTE-MARI
MAJEURE.
AT S. MARIA
MAGGIORE'S.

54. L'ÉGLISE ACCLAME NOTRE DAME DE L'ASSOMPTION.
THE CHURCH ACCLAIMS OUR LADY OF THE ASSUMPTION

(Au verso, overleaf)

55. MESSE PAPALE DE LA PROCLAMATION DU DOGME DE L'ASSOMPTION.
PAPAL MASS FOR THE PROCLAMATION OF THE DOGMA OF THE ASSUMPTION.

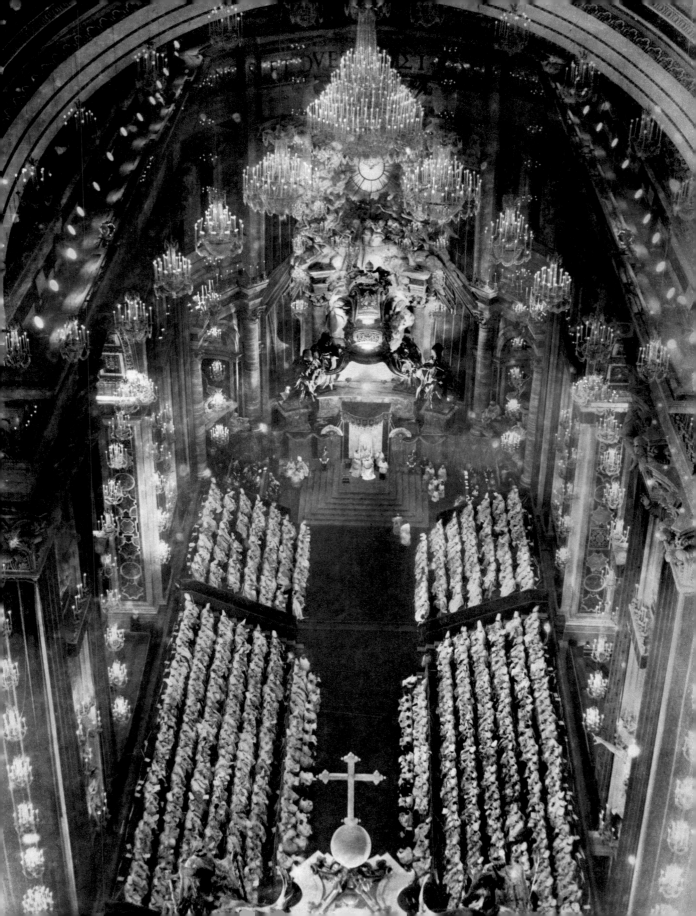

(Au recto, right-hand page)
56. VUE DE LA COUPOLE.
   SEEN FROM THE CUPOLA.

57. LE CHŒUR DE SAINT-PIERRE DURANT LA MESSE PAPALE.
SAINT PETER'S CHOIR DURING THE PAPAL MASS.

59. PAPE ET PATRIARCHE.
POPE AND PATRIARCH.

(Au recto, right-hand page)
58. MESSE EN RITE ORIENTAL DANS SAINT-PIERRE.
A MASS WITH THE ORIENTAL RITE AT SAINT PETER'S.

60. CORTÈGE PONTIFICAL DANS LA SCALA REGIA
PONTIFICAL PROCESSION IN THE SCALA REGIA

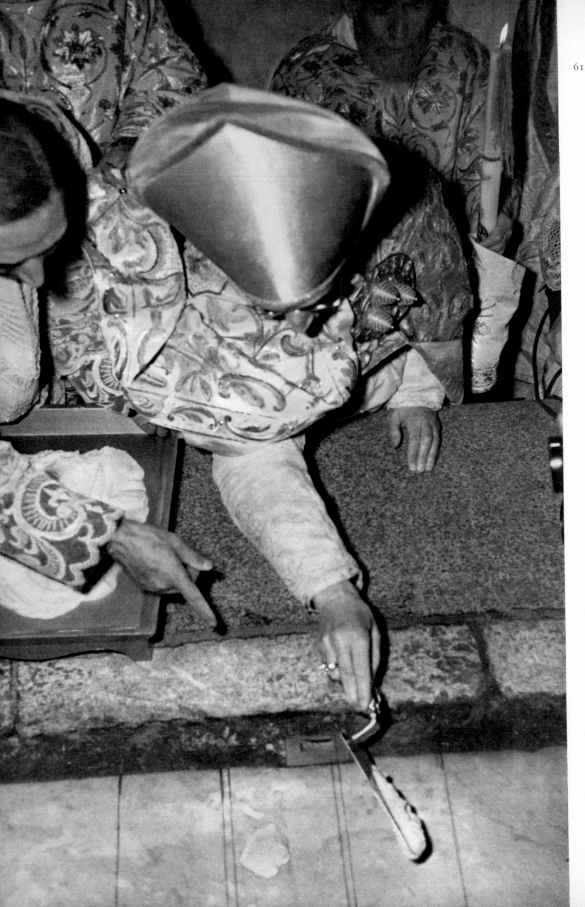

61. FERMETURE DE
LA PORTE SAINTE.
CLOSING THE
HOLY DOOR.

62. LES BRIQUES QUI
FERMENT LA
PORTE SAINTE.
THE BRICKS
WHICH SHUT UP
THE HOLY DOOR.

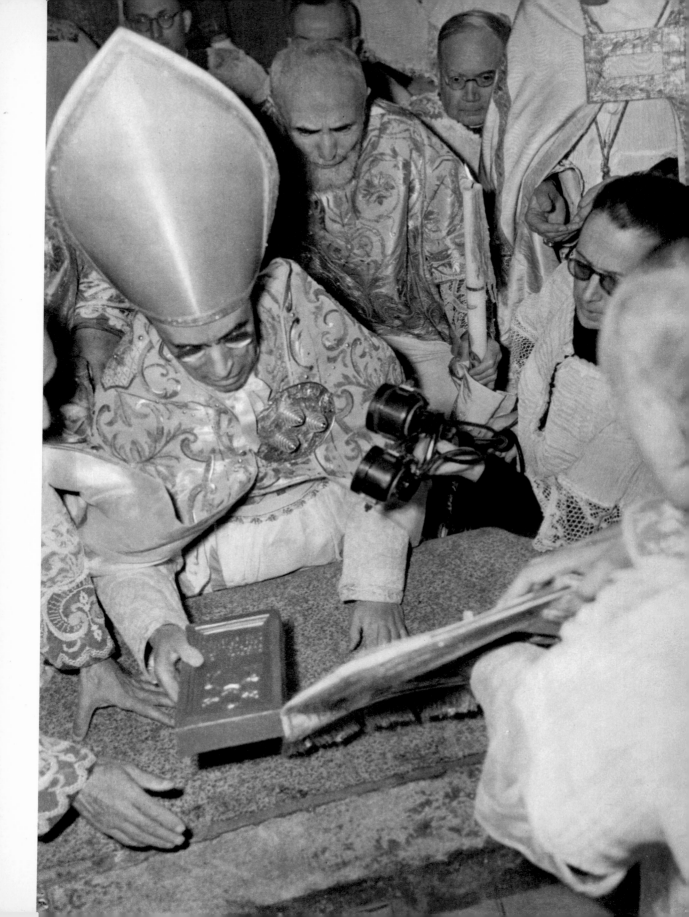

63.
SA SAINTETÉ
PRIE DEVANT
LE TOMBEAU
DE S. PIERRE.

HIS HOLINESS
PRAYING BE-
FORE SAINT
PETER'S
TOMB.

64. BÉNÉDIC
DES PALLIU
64. BLESSIN
THE PALLIU

65. BÉNÉDICTION DES AGNEAUX.
BLESSING OF THE LAMBS.

67. REMISE DE LA BARRETTE CARDINALICE.
HANDING OVER THE CARDINAL'S CAP.

68. SERMENT DES CARDINAUX
THE CARDINALS TAKING THEIR OATH

73. CONSÉCRATION DE L'ÉGLISE SAINT-EUGÈNE.
CONSECRATION OF SAINT EUGENE'S CHURCH.

74. CONSÉCRATION DE ROME AU CŒUR IMMACULÉ DE MARIE.
CONSECRATION OF ROME TO THE IMMACULATE HEART OF MARY.

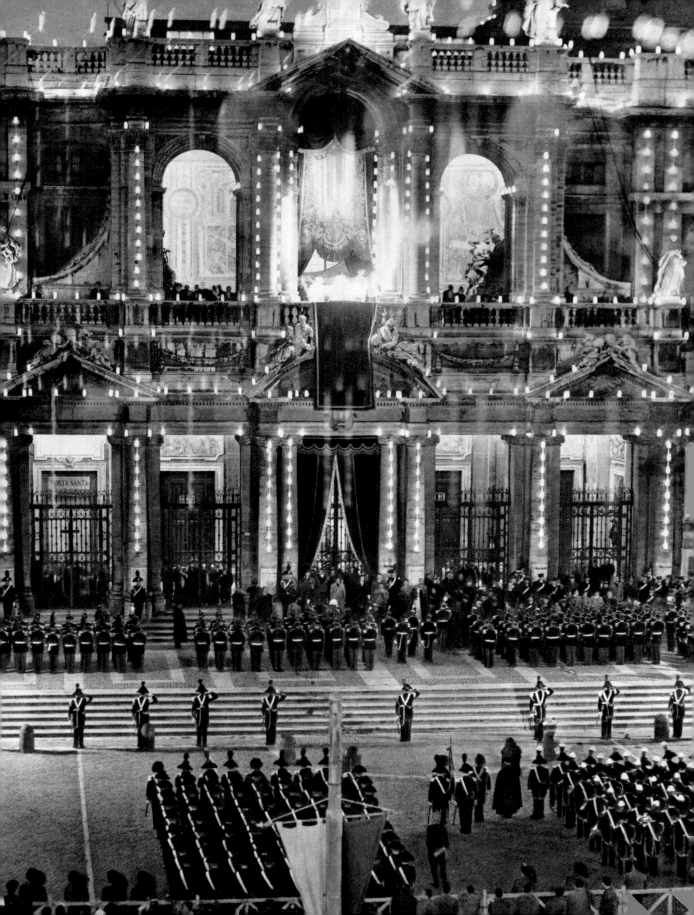

76. LA FOULE AU SOIR DU 8 DÉCEMBRE 1953.
THE CROWD, THE EVENING OF DECEMBER 8, 1953.

(Au verso, overleaf)
77. BÉNÉDICTION URBI ET ORBI.
URBI ET ORBI BLESSING.

NOTES ON THE PLATES

Frontispiece

"May the Blessing of Almighty God descend upon you."

It is the end of an audience at St Peter's. The Holy Father is borne away on the sedia to the ovations of an immense crowd which, deeply moved, is bidding its farewell after the sights and ceremonies of these last few moments— the culminating point of the pilgrimage. The beloved Pius XII has passed, but at the end of the basilica he stops the procession and his living platform, the *Bussolanti*, do a skilful half turn. He rises and his kneeling sons renew their praise, and he repeats the apostolic blessing: "*Benedicet tibi benedictionibus*— May all blessings descend upon you".

INTRODUCTION

1 THE SISTINE CHAPEL AND THE VATICAN SEEN FROM THE TOP OF THE DOME. These are the roofs of the Apostolic Palace. In the foreground, the massive Sistine Chapel looks like a fortress. It was built by Sixtus IV during the years 1475–84. Botticelli, Pinturicchio, Ghirlandaio, Rosselli, and Signorelli covered the walls with fine frescoes, and later, from 1508 to 1512, Michelangelo decorated the dome with a magnificent composition; during the years 1534–41 he executed his famous "Last Judgment" on the end wall. The entire history of humanity and all Theology is enshrined in this sanctuary of art. It is connected to the basilica and the Palace by the Royal and Ducal Halls. To the left the Belvedere Court, begun by Bramante at the end of the fifteenth century, is dominated by the Borgia Tower. Underneath the tower are Alexander VI's apartments and the Raphael rooms, whose windows face the Papagallo Court to the right. Beyond is the large Court of San Damaso, of which only the top gallery is visible, and adjoining this, the large building immediately behind it which contains the present Papal Apartments. To the left are the terraces of buildings of the Polyglot Press, the Vatican Library, *l'Osservatore Romano*, and other ancillary buildings.

2 ST PETER'S SQUARE. Set against the infinite depth of the azure sky, Michelangelo's dome crowns both the façade of the basilica (the work of Maderna in 1614) which frames the Loggia delle Benedizione and is seen through iridescent spray from the high-jetting fountain; and also the corner of Bernini's Colonnade of 1667 which leads to the Bronze Gate, the entrance to the Vatican Palace, to the Royal Staircase or Scala Regia and the Court of San Damaso.

3 THE BERNINI COLONNADE. There are 284 Doric columns and eighty-eight pilasters in the two semicircular porticoes which surround the monumental piazza of St Peter's. Bernini designed his colonnade in proportion to the gigantic new basilica. The arms of Alexander VII, and 140 graceful baroque statues adorn the upper balustrade of this severe and magnificent composition which forms the entry to the sanctuary. Ceremonies are sometimes held here owing to the size of the crowds.

4 ILLUMINATIONS ON DECEMBER 8th, 1953. It is a fantastic sight on the evenings of Easter, June 29th, or after a canonization. A thousand dancing flames of the *fiaccole* (lighted torches and incense burners containing oakum soaked in a mixture of oil, wax, and resin) vividly illuminate the dome and façade of St Peter's. All Rome comes to watch this fairy-tale scene. The first light sparkles at the Cross, then the St Peter's torch-bearers, attached to ropes controlled by winches, come down in stages, and in one perfect movement send a shower of light cascading over Michelangelo's architecture. Two or three minutes are enough. The crowd, enthralled from the very first moment, applaud in delight.
Although the electric illumination shown here is static, the effect is no less impressive. At the summit of its unique pedestal the Labarum Cross always shines resplendent through the night.

5 THE LOGGIA DELLE BENEDIZIONE AND FAÇADE OF ST PETER'S. In 1614 Maderna erected these mighty columns, five times human proportions, according to Michelangelo's rule. They frame three tiers of openings under a rather small attic, where the play of shadows is sacrificed to that of light. The façade of the basilica which conceals the interior also makes a magnificent screen 350 feet wide at the end of the vast piazza; for when the size of the crowds makes it necessary to hold ceremonies in this "greater" St Peter's, this façade serves as a reredos for the altar or as a platform for the papal throne.

6 VIEW OF THE INSIDE OF THE DOME. Over St Peter's tomb and the papal altar is Bernini's canopy, 90 feet high. The arches of the naves are 140 feet high, and the drum which admits light freely at the bottom rises to the opening of the lantern at 360 feet. Lost at the very top is the dazzling picture of God the Father as the centrepiece of the sixteen magnificently decorated sides of the dome. These also continue the upward sweep of the drum piers and show off Cavaliere de Arpino's work, in six sections underneath medallions, of the entire celestial court of Christ, the Virgin, the Apostles, the papal saints, the Angels bearing the instruments of the Passion, and the Seraphims.

Innumerable bronze stars ensure the adherence of the stucco which secures the magnificent composition of the mosaicists in this vast empyrean.

7 ONE WINDOW SHINING IN THE NIGHT. Pius XII bestowed the Blessing on the evening of the proclamation of the Dogma of the Assumption. This had been announced beforehand. The crowd which had gathered was waiting, admiring the illumination. At the appointed hour, all the lights were extinguished, and the window of the Holy Father's private apartment was opened. When he appeared he received a long ovation. This window still reveals, each night, the long vigils of our Father who works and prays for us.

8 CHRIST THE REDEEMER UNCEASINGLY BESTOWS HIS BLESSING. The façade of St Peter's is surmounted by huge statues of the Apostles, bearing the instruments of their martyrdom. In the centre, Christ leans on His Cross, His hand eternally raised in blessing of the City and the World.

9 THE POPES OF A CENTURY. Six Popes in a hundred years, venerable Sovereign Pontiffs, sanctified this palace, these halls, these chapels, this basilica. Robed in white, wearing the same sacred ornaments, they celebrated the same rites, made the same holy gestures, presided over the same assemblies in the same setting, bore the same cares, preached the same Gospel of justice, peace, and love. One heart and one spirit, they have a life that endures until the end of time, and they assure the prestige and radiance of the Papacy which, in spite of everything, is still, and more than ever, the light of the world. Whether it be Pius XII or Pius XI, Benedict XV or St Pius X, Leo XIII or Pius IX, he is the Pope, he is Peter; he is "the gentle Christ on earth". It is for Him that we go to Rome, it is His memory which these pictures of the great moments in Rome evoke, it is the Papacy which makes Rome immortal.

HIS HOLINESS PIUS XII

10 THE UNIVERSAL FATHER EMBRACES HIS SONS WHO HAVE COME FROM ALL SIDES TO HEAR HIS VOICE. These hundreds of thousands of the Faithful from all the nations have come to bring to the Vicar of Christ the tribute of their faith and love in the exultation of their Alleluiahs. It is Easter, at noon. The Holy Father, arrayed in the white damask mozetta reserved for this ceremony, repeats the message of the Resurrection before the consoling vision of Eternal Rome which the huge crowds present before him. To the left, in the distance, stretch the green horizons of the Pincio Gardens, with the Académie de

France and the Villa Medici in a small opening; and beyond the Castel Sant' Angelo, to the right, are Santa Maria Maggiore, the Capitol, and the Lateran.

11 MUNICH IN 1917. HERE IS THE FATHER'S BREAD. A poignant scene from the World War. Benedict XV, Angel of consolation and peace, sent his Nuncio to Munich. He distributed bread and other necessities to the wretched prisoners with pontifical charity. Here he is seen at the camp at Halle, on September 18th, 1918; he was at Lechfeld, on October 21st, to form a real link between the Pope and the prisoners, who afterwards recalled him vividly. The Holy See does everything in its power to comfort suffering humanity.

12 IN BUENOS AIRES IN 1934. HERE IS THE ANGELS' BREAD. Pius XI sent his Legate *"a latere"* to the American Continent, to represent him at the International Eucharistic Congress; fervent adoration of the Church before the shining monstrance of the Bread of the Spirit. A moving picture of the Eucharistic Host and the Pope—the two Christs arrayed in white.

13 AT LOURDES IN 1935. Pius XI sanctified a special jubilee for the nineteenth Centenary of the Redemption. Lourdes was chosen for a solemn meeting of the peoples at the shrine of Our Lady Co-Redemptrix. Here the Most Eminent Cardinal Legate expresses the Marian devotion of the Sovereign Pontiff. He is kneeling in the Grotto, humble and earnest, like St Bernadette, surrounded by a halo of candles. With the Immaculate Virgin, he prays for the salvation of the world. During three days and three nights Mass was celebrated on this site of miracles. The Legate sang the 140th and last Mass in the presence of 400,000 pilgrims.

14 PARIS–LISIEUX. JULY 1937. The Basilica of Sainte-Thérèse de l'Enfant Jésus had been nearly completed and had to receive the Blessing before services could be held there: the National Eucharistic Congress at Lisieux provided the occasion. Pius XI would have much liked to be there in person, but had to send his right-hand man, his Secretary of State. Here is Cardinal Pacelli on his arrival at the Gare de Lyon in Paris on July 9th, 1937. The Minister of Foreign Affairs, M. Yvon Delbos, has just welcomed him, the Republican Guards accord him military honours, the national flag is lowered before the Pope's representative, whose bearing and expression reveal depths of most noble and most holy feeling. Cardinals Verdier and Baudrillart are watching him as they stand a little in front of the crowd of Parisian notables. The next

day there was a reception by the members of the Congress at Lisieux. There were 200,000 of them on Sunday, July 11th, taking part in the Blessing of the Basilica, the Pontifical Mass, and listening to the Legate's sermon; he spoke of the Basilica, the Eucharistic Congress, and the soul of the Little Saint. A procession provided a grand finale to the day. On July 13th, after his visit to Chartres, the Cardinal was back in Paris and it was a most memorable day. From the pulpit of Notre Dame, he gave his famous sermon on "The Christian Vocation in France", and the audience could not refrain from applauding. "Here in this Church is the very Spirit of France, the Spirit of the eldest daughter of the Church, and it speaks to my spirit. Spirit of the France of today, of yesterday, of a France which goes forward in spite of everything, of a France which will never die." The ovations of the enthusiastic crowd accompanied the Legate to the Champs Élysées, the Arc de Triomphe, and the Town Hall.

"Unforgettable memories," said Cardinal Pacelli to a Prelate who reminded him, some months later, of this brilliant mission. Memories that were not forgotten! On June 11th, 1954, Cardinal Feltin, Archbishop of Paris, was the Legate for the Consecration of this basilica at Lisieux, and Pius XII broadcast a message saying: "This revives in Our heart stirring memories. It seems only yesterday, yet seventeen years have passed, since June 11th, 1937, when, as Legate to Our beloved France, it was Our happy duty to perform the inauguration and the Blessing of this same basilica, then scarcely completed."

15 ARRIVAL AT THE CONCLAVE. For nine years Secretary of State to the late Pontiff, the Cardinal Camerlengo, moved and in deep mourning, is seen returning to the Vatican after a last visit in Rome. He already lived there, but this time he was not "coming home", he was hastening to the Conclave to join his most eminent colleagues. As he stepped out of the car, his faithful chamberlain handed him his hat. An ordinary gesture of habit, perhaps, but, in the circumstances, a moment to remember. The Cardinal was the obedient son, going to meet the brethren who would designate him as the Universal Father of all the Faithful.

16 THE SEALS AFFIXED ON THE DOOR OF THE CONCLAVE. All the members of the Conclave are inside. They will be allowed no further communication with the outside world. They are meditating and praying to the Holy Spirit for guidance in their task of choosing a new successor to St Peter.

17 ELECTED POPE. MARCH 2ND, 1939. "I bring you tidings of great joy," proclaimed the First Cardinal Deacon Caccia Dominioni, on the evening of

March 2nd, 1939. "We have a Pope, the Most Eminent Cardinal Eugenio Pacelli, who has chosen to be styled Pius XII." The elected Pope, robed in one of the three white cassocks prepared for this occasion, white silk sash with gold tassels, and red velvet slippers each embroidered with a cross, wearing over the rochet the red mozzetta and stole, is seen returning to the Sistine Chapel. He is accompanied by the Master of Ceremonies, the prelates, and the dignitaries of the Pontifical Antechamber.

18 IN THE SISTINE CHAPEL AFTER HIS ELECTION. The first ceremony after the election is the dutiful submission of the cardinals. Pius XII is at the altar in the Sistine Chapel, attended by Cardinal Deacons Caccia and Canali. He is wearing the silver mitre and the *falda* (a full robe held up by two protonotaries of the "numero"—Mgr Carinci and Mgr Vitali) and a long white cope, whose orphreys are embroidered with the arms of Leo XIII. The "number" of apostolic protonotaries participating is seven. They are functionaries of the Court of Rome. The Protonotary Canons of the three Basilicas of San Giovanni in Laterano, St Peter's, and Santa Maria Maggiore are styled "supernumeraries".

19 DUTIFUL OBEISANCE OF THE CARDINALS. The Cardinals have lowered the little canopies which covered their thrones along the length of the walls of the Sistine Chapel. Only the canopy of the Elected remains, and one after the other they come to kneel before the Pope to kiss his toe, his hand, and his cheek.

20 CROWNING. MARCH 12TH, 1939. Pius XII has chosen the tiara of Pius IX for his crowning. Cardinal Caccia places it on his head, saying: "Receive the tiara with the three crowns, and know that thou art the Father of kings and princes, the Pastor of the Universe, and the Vicar on earth of Our Lord Jesus Christ, to whom be honour and glory, world without end. Amen." The triumphal ceremony takes place on the exterior balcony of St Peter's. Cardinal Gerlier, seen in profile by the throne, looking moved and happy, watches the multitudes filling the huge piazza.
In the papal ceremonies, the prelate whose function it is by right to bear and present the tiara and mitre, is the Dean of the Sacred Roman Rota, at present His Excellency Mgr André Jullien.

21 VATICAN GROTTOES. "AD CAPUT" ALTAR. His Holiness Pius XII receiving the triple crown, is invested with the powers of the primacy of St Peter, whose tomb is underneath the altar at which Pius XII has celebrated Mass for the

142

first time. One of the most important tasks of his Pontificate will be the excavation of what remains of St Peter's tomb after all these centuries. For twelve years fragments of ancient monuments were boldly excavated from under Michelangelo's dome with scrupulous care, right down to the earliest levels. These excavations have enabled scholars to write scientific treatises in support of early traditions. The monument erected over the humble grave of the martyred body of the Apostle as far back as the second century is called the "Trophy". The Emperor Constantine and the papal saint Sylvester built the basilica round this tomb, along the Vatican hillside, in spite of serious technical difficulties, proof of their determination to preserve it unchanged. Behind Constantine's Monument, which was excavated so that the marble and porphyry fragments are now visible, the Pope Saint Gregory the Great consecrated a little altar "*ad caput*", at the head of St Peter's tomb, to allow the priests to celebrate Mass on this sacred site, underneath the papal altar in the basilica. The picture shows this seventh-century altar as it was found in the excavations; in the foreground are the marble facings with which, in the fourth century, Constantine decorated the Trophy, the first ornament to be placed on the tomb of St Peter martyred in 67. The horizontal moulding visible at the top is a restoration by Calixtus II (thirteenth century). In this Chapel of the Crypt (which is called "The Clementine" because it was Clement VIII who enlarged it to its present size) doors have been cut to give access to the sides of Constantine's Monument and the Trophy. On June 29th, 1951, Pius XII consecrated the little altar enshrining these relics of the past. If one were to creep round to the right of this altar, kneel down, and lean towards the grille, one would see behind the altar part of the second-century staircase which used to lead up to the level of the little Trophy Court, chosen as the ground-level of the primitive basilica, and which is the level of the present crypt.

DIVINE OFFICES AND CEREMONIES

22 THE ANNIVERSARY "TE DEUM" AT THE LATERAN. The anniversary of the crowning is celebrated with great solemnity every year. The whole Roman Court attends a Papal Chapel, that is to say, a Mass celebrated by a cardinal in the presence of the Pope, who wears the tiara and arrives on the sedia. But on the afternoon of the following Sunday, the entire City of Rome is convened to the patriarchal arch-basilica of the Lateran for a *Te Deum* of thanksgiving and congratulation. The Cardinal Archpriest presides, surrounded by the Venerable Chapter, in the presence of the prelates of the Antechamber and

the Secretariat of State, the curates of Rome, and the delegations of the various movements of Catholic Action with their standards. In the brilliant light reflected from the gilded ceilings, the ciborium, magnificent reliquary of the Sacred Heads of Saints Peter and Paul, from the time of Urban V, gives an air of mystery to the papal altar—that ark of cypress wood containing the remains of the eucharistic table used by St Peter, and later, by the martyr popes of the early centuries. It was placed there by St Sylvester in 327.

23 THE HOLY FATHER'S PRIVATE MASS. Every morning the Holy Father celebrates Mass like a simple priest. On certain days he admits privileged people into one of the chapels in the interior of the Vatican. On the Thursday in Holy Week, the Roman Prelacy comes to take communion from his hand, when he is assisted by his Almoner, His Excellency Mgr Venini, and his Sacristan, His Excellency Mgr Van Lierde.

24 COMMUNION. At the Christmas Midnight Mass, the Holy Father celebrates Mass in the presence of the *Corps Diplomatique*. He also receives children sometimes, in a fatherly way with less ceremony, for their first Communion.

25 PREACHING. His Holiness Pope Pius XII preaches untiringly. His sermons win the admiration of the whole world. He speaks in the basilica of St Peter's, from the balcony dominating the piazza, from his apartments, and the wireless carries his firm, quiet voice far and wide. He is the living Gospel, who never ceases in his revelation of the wisdom of God to all the world, and who constantly recalls the truths and the Laws of the Church. He shows the way to the propagation of the Christian Faith, he consoles and encourages, exhorting saintliness. Here he is speaking in St Peter's from the papal altar, whose antependium is embroidered with the arms of Gregory XVI. He is wearing the mozetta and the red velvet slippers.

26 PAPAL MASS. All that humanity can boast of grandeur and beauty is gathered here around the altar where Christ is present in the voice of His Vicar. There is no more magnificent opera, in the true sense of the word, than a Papal Mass, and in this drama of the Redemption on Mount Calvary, re-enacted at the altar, the most solemn moment is the Consecration. The Dean of the Sacred College of Cardinals, Cardinal Tisserant, Bishop of Porto and St Rufino, is assisting the Holy Father. Cardinal Deacon Bruno is kneeling, and so is Mgr Dante, pontifical master of ceremonies; then there are the Archbishops attending at the throne, the privy chamberlains, the advocates of the

144

Rota, the cleric chaplains, priests, monks, seminarists, and the vast crowd, deeply moved at this moment of the Elevation. The troops on guard have obeyed the order to kneel. The silver trumpets play the inspiring harmonies of the *Harmonia Religiosa* by Silveri.

27 ON THE SEDIA. From the Paramenti Hall, where the Holy Father has put on the sacred vestments, the papal procession passes through the applauding crowd in the baroque setting of the Ducal Hall. The Palatine Guards form a line, in sombre uniform, 2nd Empire képi, epaulettes and trousers the colour of amaranth; the Noble Guards in scarlet tunics, gold cross-belts, and white breeches, surround the sedia which is borne by the "sediaries" or servants and ushers of the pontifical Antechamber—the *Bussolanti*—in crimson velvet liveries; the cardinals follow. It is March 12th, anniversary of the crowning, Pius XII is wearing the tiara and is on his way to the Sistine Chapel. The two *flabelli*, giant fans of ostrich feathers borne alongside the Pope, which will be placed on either side of the throne, are emblems of sovereignty.

28 AUDIENCE OF PRELATES. On December 24th, each year, the Roman Prelates gather in the Consistory Hall in the Holy Father's presence. The Cardinal Dean pronounces the address of vows, to which the Pope responds with the Christmas message, so momentous, so eagerly awaited, and so full of wisdom. Then each prelate approaches the throne to renew his submission and his devotion, and to receive with the Blessing a word which reaches to the very depths of his heart. Here, following the cardinals and the bishops, are the protonotary canons of the basilicas, the prelates of the Congregations and the prelates rector. Kneeling before the Holy Father is Mgr Clapperton, Rector of the Scottish Pontifical College, and standing behind him, ready to kneel, is Mgr MacMillan, Rector of the Venerable English Pontifical College.

29 AUDIENCE OF DIPLOMATS. On this same day, the *Corps Diplomatique* bring the good wishes of the nations to the Holy Father and receive on their behalf the renewed assurance of his solicitude and his prayers. His Excellency, Count Wladimir d'Ormesson, expressed his good wishes with great delicacy, and his smile shows how happy he was to hear His Holiness say: "We bless your beautiful country."

30 AUDIENCE OF PRINCES. The reception of princes and sovereigns is strictly governed by protocol. Princess Elizabeth of England and the Duke of Edinburgh were received with honour, and were accompanied by a retinue. As they passed through Raphael's rooms, and went past Swiss Guards in their

yellow doublets and breeches with red and blue slashed bands, chased
morions and halberds, they were surrounded by the prelates and private
chamberlains "of cloak and sword" in Henry II costume, wearing their
decorations, who had first received the honoured visitors and the dignitaries
of their retinue and of the British Embassy.

31 STATE AUDIENCE. The Equestrian Orders of the Holy Sepulchre and the
Knights of Malta evoke the hosts of medieval Christian Knights who dedicated their lives to the protection of holy places and the assistance of pilgrims.
The Holy Father encouraged their allegiance to the Church and their zeal
for works of charity at a general audience at St Peter's in September of the
Holy Year, 1950. Groups of pilgrims of the Franche-Comté were also present.
His Excellency Mgr Flusin, Bishop of St Claude, is seen from behind, and in
the foreground is His Excellency Mgr Dubourg, Archbishop of Besançon,
attended on his right by Mgr Pfister, French Canon of the Lateran.

32 NUNS. The Congregations of nuns have the right by Pontifical Law to the use
of a House in Rome. Here they hold meetings to elect the general superior or
to take other important decisions. At these times they seek audience with the
Holy Father to receive his encouragement and his Blessing. Here is a meeting
of the Sisters of St Joseph de Cluny as they surround the Holy Father who
is receiving them at Castelgandolfo. They have come from all over the
world, representing 3,000 nuns of their congregation. What simplicity
and paternal bounty the Sovereign Pontiff displays in his interest in their
activities!

33 MILITARY AUDIENCE. All the professions, all the arts, and all the sports have
proof of the Holy Father's solicitude and receive his familiar counsels and
wise guidance. Memories of him are touched with emotion. Soldiers are also
welcome in the Father's house when their duties take them to Rome. What
stirring memories of their Mediterranean cruise these American sailors will
take away with them!

34 AUDIENCE OF THE COMMON PEOPLE. At the end of general audiences, after the
sermon which the Holy Father preaches in the various languages of the pilgrims, the leaders of the groups and some of the leading personalities are
presented to His Holiness, who takes a friendly interest in their activities.
How graciously he turns to these peasant women in their attractive national
dress, to compliment them on the results of their work!

146

35 EXOTIC AUDIENCE. Pilgrims from the Far East, where persecution and war are rife, tell the Holy Father of their suffering countries, but also assure him of their constant fidelity to the Church. A compatriot of the College of Propaganda acts as interpreter. The Holy Father leans towards them, shocked and deeply moved. On these occasions he is indeed Father—*"Ita Pater"*.

36 LITTLE SINGERS. During the Jubilee Year and to commemorate the fiftieth anniversary of the *Motu proprio*, a letter bearing the Pope's signature and written "at his own request" which St Pius X wrote on church music, the Little Singers of the Wooden Cross and their emulators the whole world over brought their fervour and the beauty of their voices to Rome. After Mass at St Peter's, the Pope, with no regard for protocol, came to congratulate Mgr Maillet, who had conducted this school of thousands of children. As he stood amongst them, the Pope was a perfect example of "Suffer little children to come unto me".

37 FOR THE KINGDOM OF HEAVEN IS FOR SUCH. For the general audiences in the Hall of Blessings over the balcony of St Peter's, or quite often in the great Vatican basilica itself now, so numerous are the pilgrims, the Sovereign Pontiff is borne aloft on the magnificent sedia that all may see him. In spite of this enforced formality, the Holy Father's love of simplicity is revealed as his Blessing becomes a caress in response to the filial impulse of this little child.

38 THE HOLY FATHER'S PRAYER. Before the monstrance exposed at the altar of the Chair of St Peter's, Pius XII, in adoration of the Eucharistic Host, is deep in prayer and intercession for new blessings.

39 BEATIFICATION. The Rite of Beatification consists of a double ceremony. On the morning after the proclamation of the papal brief, the image of the new Blessed is uncovered at the far end of the apse in "Bernini's Glory". The crowds applaud and shout their *vivats*. A triumphal *Te Deum* follows, and the first pontifical Mass in honour of the new Blessed is then celebrated. Later the Sovereign Pontiff presides over a solemn Benediction of the Most Holy Sacrament at St Peter's.

40 PAPAL PROCESSION UNDER THE BALCONY OF ST PETER'S. The rite of Papal High Mass includes a great procession which starts from the Sistine Chapel, and descends the Scala Regia towards the great portico to enter the basilica by the central doorway. Representatives of the entire Roman regular and secular clergy are convened. They form the first group with the members of the

147

Congregation of Rites, the standards of the new saints, the Pontifical Chapel, and the Colleges of prelacy. Following them are two privy Chaplains bearing the tiara and the mitre. Next is the beginning of the procession of clergy arrayed in their ecclesiastical vestments: the Dean of the Segnatura with the censer, the youngest of the Auditors of the Rota acting as Apostolic Sub-Deacon bearing the papal Cross, then seven voters of the Segnatura acting as acolytes bearing the seven chandeliers with ornamental tapers. At the far end the dais is placed against the statue of Constantine; some of the prelates will hold the canopy over the Holy Father.

41 THE "VENI CREATOR" OF THE CANONIZATION. For the Canonization of St Pius X, such enormous crowds were anticipated that the ceremony had to be arranged in this "greater" St Peter's, the piazza. The papal throne was erected in front of the central entrance to the basilica, inside which Mass was to be celebrated by a cardinal in the Pope's presence the next day. The culminating point of the ceremony was the moment when the solemn words were pronounced: "In honour of the Holy and Indivisible Trinity, for the exaltation of the Catholic Faith and for the growth of Christian Religion, with the authority of Our Saviour Jesus Christ, the Blessed Apostles Peter and Paul and Our own; after mature deliberation and after frequently imploring the divine help, and counsel with our venerable brethren the Cardinals of the Holy Roman Church, the Patriarchs, Archbishops and Bishops present in the city, We decree and define as Saint, and we inscribe in the list of saints the Blessed Pius X, Confessor." But the moment immediately preceding was the most moving. The Sovereign Pontiff was kneeling and the huge crowd prayed with him in silence. This reverent and devoted silence was inexpressibly solemn. Then the *Veni Creator* was intoned and the crowd rose, impatient to show praise and thanksgiving in the *Te Deum*.

42 PAPAL CHAPEL SERVICE IN HONOUR OF ST PIUS X. The day after May 29th His Eminence the Cardinal Dean of the Sacred College, Eugene Tisserant, in the name of the Holy Father and in his presence celebrated pontifical Mass at the Papal Altar. The crowd, the illuminations, and the singing lent incomparable splendour to this ceremony. Here is the papal procession leaving the basilica of St Peter's, to proceed to the loggia outside, whence the Sovereign Pontiff will give his Blessing to the Faithful who have not been able to find room in the vast basilica. Outside and in, the scene is awe-inspiring. The crowds welcome the Vicar of Jesus Christ, and heads are bowed as he raises his hand in blessing. They are moved to the depths of their hearts, and eyes are wet with tears. Souls are aroused to a desire for saintliness or

are converted. The silver trumpets in the *Hymne Papal* by Gounod do not entirely drown the storm of applause. Thoughts of eternal beatitude and celestial joy are evoked.

43 THE SHRINE OF ST PIUS X AT THE PAPAL ALTAR. After the Canonization the shrine of St Pius X was unveiled at the papal altar, where he had celebrated Mass, above the tomb of the first papal saint, whose Confession was surely never more victorious. The hundred lights which constantly burn at St Peter's today honour his 258th successor, enrolled after him in the list of Saints. Many flowers adorn the altar.

Cardinal Tisserant is celebrating the Mass of the Papal Chapel of May 30th, 1954. Crowds surround the altar. The standard depicting the miracle of François Belsani, the lawyer of Naples, who lay dying of cancer of the lung and was instantaneously cured on August 26th, 1952, hangs from St Veronica's balcony. Opposite is the picture of a Sister of St Vincent de Paul who was cured on February 14th in this same year 1952. It was these two instances of healing after the Beatification, which were both recognized as miracles, that admitted the Canonization.

44 TRIDUUM FOR ST PIUS X AT SANTA MARIA MAGGIORE. A more imposing tribute has never been seen than that paid to St Pius X by the City of Rome on the evening of May 30th, 1954. A great procession of men and boys bore the revered shrine from St Peter's to Santa Maria Maggiore, crossing the Capitol in the midst of great multitudes of people, whose single-hearted devotion was most impressive. As in the early centuries, it was indeed a case of canonization by popular acclaim. As night fell, the shrine was reaching the Esquiline Hill. In the illuminated basilica the cardinals received it and accompanied it to the altar. From left to right are Cardinals Gerlier, Aloisi-Masella, Micara, Van Roey, Tedeschini, Agagianian, Roncalli, and Feltin. For three days solemn ceremonies were held, then, until the end of the week, there was an unceasing flow of reverent crowds to worship at the shrine. Thus the Marian Year reached its culminating point.

SPECIAL OCCASIONS OF THE LAST FIFTEEN YEARS

45 THE "POSSESSO" AT SAN GIOVANNI IN LATERANO. For ten centuries the Popes resided at the Patriarchate of the Lateran and the Basilica of the Holy Saviour, and of the two, San Giovanni has remained the papal cathedral *"Omnium*

ecclesiarum mater et caput". The new Pontiff, Bishop of Rome, must at the earliest opportunity come to take possession of his throne. At the Celebration of the Ascension on May 18th, 1939, Pius XII performed this traditional rite. It was his first public appearance in Rome, and great crowds of the Faithful had gathered. He is seen here as the *Te Deum* is being sung; he is being borne aloft on the sedia and has just received the keys of the basilica. He is about to celebrate papal Mass at the altar of Confession, surrounded by cardinals, bishops, the clergy of the Lateran, members of the pontifical Court, and the *Corps Diplomatique*. It is the highest ceremony which can be held in the venerable cathedral of cathedrals, at the end of which the Benediction *Urbi et Orbi* is pronounced from the balcony outside. A consoling sight as well as magnificent, both for the Holy Father as he sees and feels the devotion of his spiritual children, and for the Faithful who are happy as they watch the benevolent expression and loving gestures of this universal Father, and know that they are "all one in Christ".

46 PAPAL BLESSING FROM THE BALCONY OF THE LATERAN. It was for this solemn ceremony which concludes the Papal Mass that Galilei constructed this mighty façade, 180 feet wide, under the pontificate of Clement XII in 1735. It is one of the finest façades in the world, conceived on a human scale, yet with a dignity worthy of the majesty of the "basilica mother of churches". It is a magnificent setting, showing off the loggia to the best advantage. In the centre above the principal entrance, the balcony of the upper balustrade projects, surrounded by four massive columns, which rise from their sculptured bases in one sweep to support the triangular crowning tympanum. The entrances on either side with their balconies and pillars are slightly recessed, as is the baroque cyma supporting the statues of the Doctors of the Church, dominated by a colossal statue of the Saviour, at a height of more than 150 feet. There could be no more splendid setting for pontifical sovereignty.

47 OPENING THE HOLY DOOR. The five patriarchal basilicas of Rome each have one door, called the Holy Door, which is normally walled up and is only opened during Jubilee Years, great occasions sanctioned every twenty-five years. The Pope presides in person over this opening of the Door for the Holy Year on December 24th. The Sovereign Pontiff knocks three times with a precious hammer and the brick wall, previously loosened, falls in one piece on to a trolley and is rapidly wheeled into the interior.

48 THE OPENED DOOR. During a psalm of joy—*Jubilate Deo omnis terra*—the Penitentiaries wash the threshold and the stiles of the Holy Door with sponges

dipped in Holy Water. The Holy Father then chants an orison. He kneels, intones the *Te Deum*, and is the first to enter by the Holy Door, followed by the cardinals and the whole crowd, the beginning of the constant stream which continues throughout the Holy Year.

49 THE HOLY DOOR OF THE LATERAN. At the same time, the cardinal legates open the Holy Doors of the other basilicas with the same rites. Under the vast portico of the Lateran, the magnificent ceremony unfolds; the procession starts from the Scala Sancta, a nearby sanctuary famous for the Holy Staircase of the Praetorium of Jerusalem brought by Constantine, which may only be ascended in a kneeling position. The procession descends the slope of the square to return by the central path through the lawns and the great parvis. The ivory and silver-gilt hammer was presented to Pius XI by the French Catholic Youth Movement. The wall had been erected at the end of the Jubilee of the Redemption of 1933, and now three knocks caused it to fall slowly back in one movement.

50 THE CARDINAL LEGATE MICARA AT THE LATERAN. The Legate at the Lateran is His Eminence Cardinal Clement Micara. The Holy Door is now open, and like the Holy Father at St Peter's, he is the first to enter the patriarchal basilica on the Pope's behalf, followed by the Venerable Chapter who are attending him, and by huge crowds of the Faithful who crowd in behind him. For a whole year entry here will be continuous.

51 JUBILEE VISIT TO SAN GIOVANNI IN LATERANO. During August of the Holy Year, His Holiness Pius XII returned to Rome—"Pilgrim from Castel-gandolfo"—to join the Faithful who thronged the Holy Doors of the great basilicas. A pious crowd had gathered on the square around the Lateran and filled the vast patriarchal basilica. The Holy Father steps out of his car, attended by the prelates of his Antechamber, Mgr Arboria Mella di Sant' Elia and Mgr Calori di Vignale, and he is received by His Excellency Mgr Di Jorio, Vicar of the Cardinal Archpriest, who is bowing before His Holiness, while the Venerable Chapter awaits him on the parvis. In the background are the remains of the ancient Popes' Palace: it is the "Sancta Sanctorium", basilica of San Lorenzo, the private chapel of the Popes for a thousand years, celebrated for its relics and for the miraculous *"achéiropoïète"* icon of St Saviour at the top of the Scala Sancta. The fine mosaic is still visible in the apse of the Triclinium, or great hall, depicting Leo III's reception of Charlemagne, in the year 800. In the centre is Christ among the Apostles. On the left, Christ gives the keys to St Sylvester and the vexillum to Constantine.

On the right, St Peter, hanging on the Cross, offers the pallium to Leo III and an oriflamme to Charlemagne.

52 JUBILEE VISIT TO SAN PAULO FUORI LE MURA. Continuing his visits to gain the Jubilee Indulgence, the Pope, enveloped in vast purple robes and surrounded by ceremonial officials and Noble Guards, proceeds to San Paulo fuori le Mura. He passes along the fine colonnade, blessing the Faithful who have gathered to join his august prayer.

53 AT SANTA MARIA MAGGIORE. Seminarists from Asia, Africa, and America have come to join in procession with the Holy Father as he enters the venerable sanctuary, the first in the Eternal City to be dedicated to the Virgin Mary, Mother of God, and which was the centre of devotion during the Marian Jubilee. The prelates of the pontifical Antechamber and the members of the Chapter crowd around Pius XII, who is so devoted to the Virgin Mary.

54 THE CHURCH ACCLAIMS OUR LADY OF THE ASSUMPTION. On November 1st, 1950, a very rare, and therefore the more stirring, ceremony was held for the proclamation of the Dogma of the Assumption of the Holy Virgin Mary. His Holiness Pius XII has described this day: "A luminous morning, of unusual and mysterious splendour." The morning mist lent all the more radiance to the sun when it finally burst forth, just as the Sovereign Pontiff, on the sedia and under the canopy, came out through the Bronze Door, at the end of a long procession. It was remarkable that all at once the crescent moon high in the sky shone astonishingly clear. In front of the great basilica, the square had become the "greater" St Peter's.

55 PAPAL MASS FOR THE PROCLAMATION OF THE DOGMA OF THE ASSUMPTION. On this morning of the extraordinary All Saints' Day of 1950, it was quite impossible to move in the crowd of more than half a million. The majority chose to watch the rite of the definition of the dogma outside the basilica. Those who filled the interior were able to hear the Pope's voice through loud-speakers, and, in this setting, as thrilling as it was awe-inspiring, they could watch his processional entry and the Mass in which the new text was followed for the first time. It is the supreme moment of the Consecration. All are kneeling, and the Noble and Swiss Guards are giving a military salute.

56 VIEW FROM THE DOME. A lofty view taken from the gallery of the dome. The

gigantic proportions of the building and the size of the enormous crowd can be seen.

57 THE CHOIR OF ST PETER'S SEEN DURING HOLY MASS. On November 1st, 1950, the whole Catholic world was united in thought with those who had been able to come to the special ceremony. Eight hundred bishops surrounded the Sovereign Pontiff during Papal Mass, giving the impression of an oecumenical council in the apse of St Peter's.

58 A MASS WITH THE ORIENTAL RITES AT ST PETER'S. His Beatitude Maxim IV Saïgh, Patriarch of the Melchites of Antioch, together with fourteen archbishops and bishops, celebrates pontifical mass, following the Byzantine liturgy in the presence of the Sovereign Pontiff, who participates from a throne erected in front of the great square altar for this special rite, and pronounces the Blessings in Greek. The Orientals, arrayed in their splendid liturgical vestments, are shown in the picture as each is censing the Eucharist which he has just consecrated.

59 POPE AND PATRIARCH. The celebrating Patriarch, who wears the oriental episcopal crown, assures the Pope, who wears the tiara, of his homage and obedience. It is the moment when His Holiness reaches the apse of the basilica, carried on the high throne in the processional entry.

60 PONTIFICAL PROCESSION IN THE SCALA REGIA. For the great papal ceremonies at the Basilica of St Peter's, the abbots, bishops, and archbishops present in Rome are invited to form a procession to the Sovereign Father who is on the *sedia gestatoria* and is surrounded by archbishops attending at the throne, by the Sacred College of Cardinals, and by the whole court of prelates and laymen. They all wear ecclesiastical vestments and each carries a lighted taper.

61 SEALING THE HOLY DOOR. For a whole year, innumerable faithful worshippers had entered the basilica by this door to gain the Jubilee Indulgence. On Sunday, December 24th, 1950, with the same solemnity as for the opening ceremony, the Pope performed the Sealing of the Door. He entered for the last time, and after praying in the interior, he was the last to come out by this Door. The pink granite steps were removed and the Holy Father blessed the bricks and lime. He knelt at the threshold and, with a precious trowel, placed the mortar at certain marked points, repeating Christ's words: "Thou art Peter, and on this Stone will I found My Church". At the same time, similar

ceremonies were performed by the Cardinal Legates at the Lateran, Santa Maria Maggiore, and San Paulo.

62 THE BRICKS WHICH WALL UP THE HOLY DOOR. The Sovereign Pontiff places a gilded brick between two silver bricks, saying that the Door must not be opened until the next Jubilee Year. He prays God to protect this holy place where the Faithful have received so many mercies. A temporary partition is immediately erected. There is a certain note of regret as the thanksgiving *Te Deum* is sung, that this thrilling year has come to an end for Rome. The Jubilee will continue for another year, celebrated throughout the world.

63 ST PETER'S DAY, HIS HOLINESS PIUS XII PRAYS AT THE APOSTLE'S TOMB. During the vigil on the eve of St Peter's Day, the Holy Father goes down to the open Confession of the basilica to worship the Apostle. His Holiness Pius XII, St Peter's successor, meditates on this sacred site, which, thanks to him, is now better known. The recent excavations revealed that the ground in this part of the Confession is directly above the little court where the earliest Christians used to gather before the Trophy, the monument over St. Peter's tomb. It was constructed in the form of a niche in the second century, and was discovered under many layers of marble and mosaic decorations. Framing the top of the recess is an iron grille, which was not covered up by the seventeenth-century marbles, and through which fine Limoges enamels can be seen, proof of the unceasing devotion of the Faithful.

64 BLESSING OF THE PALLIUMS. After praying at St Peter's tomb, on the evening of June 28th, the Sovereign Pontiff blesses the Palliums. These are special liturgical vestments conferred on archbishops and on certain bishops according to their diocese or personal status. The Pallium is a white woollen stole, embroidered with black crosses, the ends hanging down the chest and the back. One of the little black crosses can be seen between the Holy Father and the book which His Excellency Mgr Venini is holding before His Holiness, who is attended by His Excellency Mgr the Sacristan Van Lierde and the pontifical masters of ceremonies, Mgr Dante and Mgr Bonazzi. The Palliums blessed in this way are preserved in a gilded urn which is kept in the Trophy, before which the Holy Father has just been praying, and which, until the recent excavations, was only known as "the Niche of the Palliums". In the previous picture (63), the corner of this coffer decorated with heads of cherubims in the clouds can be seen. It is from this niche that the Sacred Palliums are fetched when the Holy Father confers them in the Consistory Court.

65 BLESSING OF THE LAMBS. The Sacred Palliums are woven with the wool of two lambs, presented each year by the Cistercian Abbey of San Paulo delle Tre Fontane and brought to Pontifical Mass at the Basilica of Sant' Agnese in the Via Nomentana on January 21st, St. Agnes' Day, and then presented by the Chapter of the Lateran for the Blessing of the Holy Father. The lambs are crowned and adorned with flowers, and one is decorated with white ribbon and the other with red. His Excellency the Dean of the Rota, two Canons of the Lateran, with their masters of ceremonies, two Cistercian Monks, and the Dean of the Consistorial Advocates take part in this ceremony, which is directed by the Prefect of the Pontifical ceremonies.

66 IMPOSITION OF THE PALLIUMS BY CARDINAL TISSERANT. On the day after the Consistory, when the Palliums have been solicited and conferred, the first Cardinal Deacon celebrates Mass in the Matilda or Paulina Chapel for the imposition of this emblem in the presence of archbishops or their procurators. His Eminence Cardinal Tisserant, Dean of the Sacred College, used to perform this rite when he belonged to the Order of Deacons, before he was appointed to the suburbicarian bishopric of Porto and Santa Rufina, where he has recently built and consecrated a cathedral.

67 HANDING OVER THE BIRETTA. In 1946 His Holiness Pius XII had already filled the Sacred College by creating thirty-two cardinals according to oecumenical promotion and the number of nations honoured, however distant. It was the same in 1953. The names were published on November 30th, 1952. There were twenty-four, two of whom were from the "Silent Church". On the evening of January 14th, 1953, the handing over of the birettas took place at a secret Consistory in the Tronetto Hall. Here is the Archbishop of Montreal, His Eminence Cardinal Léger, kneeling before the Holy Father as the biretta is placed on his head.

68 THE CARDINALS' OATH. At the beginning of the Public Consistory of January 15th, 1953, the existing cardinals took their places in the apse of St Peter's, while the new cardinals were in the Chapel of St Petronilla, where they took the oath prescribed by the Code. Shortly afterwards, the cardinal deacons came to conduct them to the Holy Father who imposed the Cardinals' Hats.

69 IMPOSITION OF THE CARDINAL'S HAT AT ST PETER'S. This is the most characteristic rite in the creation of a cardinal. Each one in turn goes up to the throne to kneel before the Sovereign Pontiff who is seated and is wearing the mitre.

The Pope places the wide flat hat with the long silk tassels on the head, already covered by the cappa, and says: "Receive this emblem of the dignity of the cardinalate, which signifies that you must show yourself intrepid for the exaltation of the holy Faith, the peace and tranquillity of Christian peoples, and the conservation and growth of the Holy Roman Church, even to the shedding of blood if need be." Their Eminences responded with a most heartfelt *Amen*.

70 IMPOSITION OF THE CARDINAL'S HAT AT CASTELGANDOLFO. The Nuncios who had been raised to this office in November 1952 were to receive the biretta on January 14th, 1953, from the hands of the Sovereign, and thereafter they were representatives of the Holy See and could not be in Rome on the following day. A special consistory was held while the Holy Father was in residence at Castelgandolfo. Among the cardinals present at this more private ceremony, here is Cardinal Roncalli as the Holy Father places the Cardinal's Hat on his head. He had received the biretta at the Élysée, and had left the Nunciature in Paris for the Patriarchate of Venice.

71 THE CARDINALS' PRAYER AT THE CONFESSION OF ST. PETER'S. A thrilling moment: after all the honours which they have received, the new cardinals show their devotion and their thanksgiving to the great martyr Apostle, St Peter, founder of the Roman Church. They are kneeling, like pilgrims, around the open Confession in front of the Papal altar over the humble grave in which the first Pope was laid to rest on the evening of his martyrdom.

BISHOP OF ROME

72 DEFENSOR CIVITATIS. JULY 19TH AND AUGUST 13TH, 1943. Rome knew the horrors of death and destruction by bombing from the air. Great columns of smoke hung over the stricken areas. The Holy Father was the first to arrive at the scene of disaster. The moment he arrived the crowd surrounded him. In a white overcoat and hatless, he was the bishop among his diocesans. He distributed all that he had managed to gather together to succour them in their distress, as they cried: "I have lost everything." "Four of my family are dead." "My house has been destroyed." The crowds pressed about him as he went. Before the Basilica of San Lorenzo, he knelt on the rubble and prayed for the dead, repeating the *Pater* and the *Ave*. They all joined in the responses. He gave blessings, consolation, and encouragement. Here he is shown in

front of the basilica of San Giovanni in Laterano; to his right is Mgr Montini, to his left, Mgr Nasali Rocca. All these men and boys are still stunned, and the women weeping. When he wished to continue on his way, his car would not start, and the boys pushed it, forming a new sedia. Mgr Respighi conducted this heroic ceremony. A new pact of fidelity was sealed between Rome and her Pastor. Also, it was he who would obtain her freedom without destructive fighting. He defends and preserves the City.

73 CONSECRATION OF THE CHURCH OF ST EUGENE. The Pope is the Bishop of Rome. His Cardinal-Vicar represents him at all the current episcopal functions. But His Holiness Pius XII constantly looks to the spiritual welfare of Rome, which he would wish to set high standards for all the world. For his jubilee, a church was presented to him, with the name of his Patron Saint, St Eugene. He graciously consecrated the High Altar, encouraging the engineers and artists, and thanking the benefactors who help him to build churches in new areas. The Holy Father is here seen praying, during the burning of the five little wax and incense crosses on the place which he has just anointed with the Holy Oils. The vast church is in the beautiful Via Flaminia area, in a modern eighteenth-century style.

ROME, THE MARIAN CITY

74 CONSECRATION OF ROME TO THE IMMACULATE HEART OF THE VIRGIN. Rome truly deserves to be known as the Marian City. How cheering is the manifest piety of the people before the local shrines of the Madonna, which, at street corners or against walls, like the one at Castro Pretorio, receive continual homage of prayers, greetings, or offerings of candles and flowers; wishes or thanksgivings, often written on ex-voto tablets. There are certain memorable days, particularly the day of the solemn Consecration of Rome to the Immaculate Heart of the Virgin before the church of Aracoeli, a municipal parish on the Capitol. In the presence of crowds which filled the vast spaces of the Piazza di Venezia, Piazzo San Marco, and the Via del Mare, the Pope pronounced the Consecration at the feet of the Madonna. In this Marian Year, the anniversary was marked by a very beautiful renovation ceremony. The picture shows the crowd in front of the ancient façade, which looks more like a fortress but clearly defines the naves of the basilica. Its beauty lies in the interior, with its many monuments, evoking memories of the centuries.

75 SANTA MARIA MAGGIORE, WHICH, WITH LOURDES, IS THE CENTRE OF THE MARIAN YEAR. The encyclical letter *Fulgens Corona*, "The Radiant Crown"— the Pope's Apostolic Letters addressed to all Christian peoples are always referred to by their opening words—had announced a special world-wide Jubilee on the occasion of the centenary of the definition of the Dogma of the Immaculate Conception. For the opening of this Marian Year, fixed for December 8th, 1953, His Holiness Pius XII went to the basilica of Santa Maria Maggiore to read a prayer of his own composing before the Madonna, "The Salvation of the People of Rome". There was a tremendous ovation from the whole crowd. The troops in close ranks presented arms. Here are the troops of honour with standards. On the square are the Italian Carabinieri, and on the parvis the Palatine Guard, in front of the façade of the Basilica and the balcony which the Pope has just reached.

For the illumination, an ingenious electric installation was devised to give the illusion of the *fiaccole* of olden days. An alternating automatic lighting-up arrangement gave the effect of flames quivering in the wind. Every evening of this year 1954, the façade and the campanile shone through the night, inviting prayer. There was an incessant flow of pilgrims to this place of worship.

76 THE CROWD ON THE EVENING OF DECEMBER 8TH. There were crowds all along the papal procession and on the Piazza di Spagna, but chiefly in front of the basilica, in the long Carlo Alberto and Merulana Streets, which connect Santa Maria Maggiore to S. Croce in Gerusalemme and to San Giovanni in Laterano.

77 BLESSING "URBI ET ORBI". After the ceremony which groups of young girls in white attended in the interior of Santa Maria Maggiore, the Holy Father came to the balcony to give the Blessing to the City and the World. On this evening a beautiful and holy page was written in the history of Rome.

This is the text of the Pope's Blessing:

Sancti Apostoli Petrus et Paulus de quorum potestate et auctoritate confidimus, ipsi intercedant pro vobis ad Dominum.

Amen

May the Holy Apostles Peter and Paul, in whose power and authority we trust, intercede for you with the Lord.

Amen

Precibus et meritis beatæ Mariæ semper Virginis, beati Michaelis

Through the prayers and the merits of the Blessed Virgin Mary,

158

Archangeli, beati Joannis Baptistæ et sanctorum Apostolorum Petri et Pauli, et omnium Sanctorum: Misereatur vestri omnipotens Deus et dimissis omnibus peccatis vestris, perducat vos Jesus Christus ad vitam æternam.

Amen

Indulgentiam, absolutionem et remissionem omnium peccatorum vestrorum, spatium veræ et fructuosæ poenitentiæ, cor semper poenitens, et emendationem vitæ, gratiam et consolationem Sancti Spiritus et finalem perseverantiam in bonis operibus tribuat vobis omnipotens et misericors Dominus.

Amen

Et benedictio Dei omnipotentis, Patris et Filii et Spiritus Sancti descendat super vos et maneat semper.

Amen

of Blessed Michael the Archangel, Blessed John the Baptist and the Holy Apostles Peter and Paul and of all the Saints: may Almighty God have mercy upon you, forgive you your sins, and may Jesus Christ bring you to everlasting life.

Amen

May the Almighty and most merciful God grant you forgiveness, absolution and remission of all your sins, time for a true and worthy penance, an ever-penitent heart, and true amendment of life, the grace and consolation of the Holy Spirit and final perseverance in good works.

Amen

And may the blessing of Almighty God, the Father, the Son and the Holy Ghost come down upon you and remain with you always.

Amen

ACKNOWLEDGEMENTS

All the photographs in this book were taken by M. G. Felici, the Papal Photographer at Rome, with the exception of the following: 6 and 8 (the Author); 21 (Rev. Fabbrica di San Pietro in Vaticano); 31, 35, 42, 54, 56–7, 68 (Foto Attualita Giordani, Rome); 12 (*El Pueblo*, Buenos Aires); 1–3, 5 (M. A. Trincano, Lyons); 14 (Union Française Photographique, Paris); 33 (United Press Association, New York); 13 (Photo Viron, Lourdes).